PLAN B

*How Real People are Using the
Internet to Create a
Second Income*

DEBORAH H. ROBERTSON

Interior Design: Charles Sutherland

ISBN: 13:978-1499315653
10:1499315651

Published by: Create Space

The websites referred to in this book are not the property of Deborah Robertson and may change at any time.

First Edition

For additional copies, visit:
www.FollowDeborah.com

REGISTER YOUR BOOK

AND ACCESS FREE ONLINE MARKETING
RESOURCES FROM DEBORAH

Don't forget to register your book to gain access to some private resources Deborah has put together to help you start an online business quickly.

RECEIVE a subscription to Deborah's online marketing newsletter so you know exactly what's working now and what's not. Plus, get access to some private training Deborah has put together to get you off to a fast start.

COMPLETE a questionnaire and Deborah will set up a FREE strategy session with you to determine if your idea for an online business is viable or not. You can also use this $250 session to get personal help from Deborah on an existing online business that you already have.

Visit FOLLOWDEBORAH.COM/REGISTER to
access the above resources.

DEDICATION

To my Mom, Frances Henderson, who is my hero. She is the one who has always believed in me, encouraged me, trained me up in the way I should go, loved me unconditionally, and has been my inspiration throughout my life.

To my husband, who just lets me be me. It doesn't matter where I am flying off to or what new adventure I am starting, he is always supportive.

To my amazing grandchildren—Austin, Baylee, Jordan, Cam, Cade, Madison, and Braydon, who will accomplish their dreams in life whether it is to become a professional dancer, a professional ballplayer, a doctor, a pilot, an emergency responder, or any other endeavor. All that is needed is having the right mindset and taking the right action steps to move you in that direction. Never quit when it seems the obstacles are just too great. Find a way to push through and keep on moving forward. Never give up.

To my children, Steven and Stacie—you are never too old to think "outside" the box.

To my MOBE community, who is always a source of encouragement. To Matt Lloyd, founder of MOBE, for providing the training that has taken me on a journey that I never dreamed possible.

To my friend David Dutton for his encouragement, support, and guidance through the entire process of writing this book.

To my friends Carolina Millan, Rob Tepper, Rob Paris, Mike and Tammy Morin, Helen Avery, Scott Ewart, Andrea Goodsaid, my "case studies" who were kind enough to allow me to include their online successes as a part of this book.

Introduction

Most people ask the question, "What am I going to do?" after they lose a job. However, the time to be asking that question is before you lose a job, not afterward. In the 1960s, people built bomb shelters due to the threat of the Cold War. They built them in anticipation of "What if . . . ?" Waiting to build a bomb shelter until after a bomb had been dropped would have been too late. They were prepared for the worst case scenario, and thank goodness that scenario never played out.

My hope is the same for you—that the scenario of your job disappearing tomorrow will never come to fruition.

But . . . there are no guarantees. So, my question is, "What is your bomb shelter? What is your plan?"

Most people don't have one. They simply continue to struggle with their income not keeping up with the cost of living, just hoping that their job will always be there.

Most people probably never think about what they would do if their job suddenly disappeared tomorrow. It's almost the mentality that it may happen to someone else, but not to me. The reality is that it could happen to anyone at any time. It doesn't matter if you're in the public or private sector. Job security is a thing of the past.

So what do I recommend you do? Plan, plan, plan. Plan for what if you walked into work tomorrow, and you were told that you were no longer needed. What would be your Plan B? What options could you consider? Just think about some of them.

Ask people what they would do if they lost their job today and most would say they would go straight to the unemployment office. That would help, but it certainly won't keep you at the standard of living you are accustomed to, and then it's limited. So during that time, what would you do? Probably . . .

1. Get your resume in order and start job hunting.

2. Go back to school and re-invent yourself with a new skill.

So, let's say you are successful. You are able to re-invent yourself or find another job.

When will that cycle end? When will the next layoff occur? The problem with these choices is that they keep you in the same never-ending cycle. Someone else always has the control over your income and your lifestyle.

Do you sometimes feel like you're a hamster on its wheel? It runs and runs, goes around and around as fast as it can go, but never really goes anywhere. If I had to do it all over again, what would I do knowing what I know now? I would start my own business while I worked at my regular job. But not just any business. I would have a business that gives me freedom. I would have an online business.

What kind of freedom do most people want? Most people want the freedom to live life on their own terms, but they don't want to do what it takes for that to happen. Most people will tell you their ideal life is to be able to do what they want to do when they want to do it and for money never to be an issue.

In today's world, that type of freedom is entirely possible. People are creating their own wealth and not waiting for someone else to tell them how much they should be paid. The Internet has changed many aspects of how the world does business. You can now work from anywhere in the world with just a computer (or even a smartphone) and an Internet connection. Having a job that would not require you to be anywhere at any particular time for money to flow—that is what real freedom is all about.

With the Internet, you can virtually start your home business today and have customers all over the world by tomorrow.

With the Internet, your resources are limitless. Your potential is infinite.

You may ask, "How do I start an online business?"

Well, there are some questions you must ask yourself. First, you must determine what you want to do.

1. Do you want to sell your own products?
2. Do you want to sell someone else's products (become an affiliate)?
    a. Do you become an affiliate for low-cost products (with low-end commissions)?
    b. Do you become an affiliate for top-tier products (with high-end commissions)?
3. Do you have a service that you can provide online?
4. Do you have training that you can provide online?

It doesn't matter if you're in the online world or the offline world, the only way people make money is if someone gives it to them in exchange for a product, a service, or training.

Think of when you give money to people offline.

You buy a product. You go to a retail store and you buy something tangible, like shoes, and you give the clerk money.

You buy a service. You go to the dentist and have your teeth cleaned, and you give the dentist money (and a lot of it!).

You pay for an institution to teach you to become a teacher, a doctor, or a lawyer (education/training).

It works the same way online. . . . except now people are giving you money for your product, your service, or your training.

Building a business, whether online or offline, takes time, patience, and a lot of creativity. Give yourself at least one year to get established in your online business and to be making the kind of money you want to make. You can't treat it like a hobby; you must treat it like a business.

In this book, you will learn the ways that people make money online through selling products, services, or training. My hope is that in reading this book and in studying the "case studies" of those who have been successfully making money online, that you will see an online business as a viable solution to give you the freedom in your life that you desire.

But don't wait until you no longer have a job to get started. Think what your life would look like if you had even a few hundred dollars extra each month. Then think about what your life would look like if you had a few thousand dollars extra a month, or even tens of thousands of dollars extra each month.

These are real possibilities, and throughout this book, you'll discover ways that people are making it happen for them every day.

Be encouraged and always stay the course. Your life is about to change.

Table of Contents

1

7 Good Reasons Why an Online Business Makes Perfect Sense

1. Low Start-Up Cost

While owning a proven franchise like a McDonalds would be awesome, it's just not feasible for most people. However, an online business is in reach of most would-be entrepreneurs, because for just a few hundred dollars or less, you can be in business.

The basics that you need to start an online business are a domain name, a hosting account to host your website, some graphics to make your site look nice, and I would add an autoresponder to capture leads that come to your website. You can start out very simple and add on or improve as you have the funds to do so.

2. Open 24/7

The great thing about an online business is that while one part of the world is sleeping, there is another part of the world doing business. When you open an online business, you can be open 24/7 if you like.

3. Time Freedom

One of the awesome benefits of an online business is that once you get up and running, you can actually take more time off from the business if you want to. The work that you have done days, weeks, and even months ago will build on itself. The traffic will continue to grow as will your e-mail list. Typically, as these two items grow, so will sales.

4. Easy to Find Your Target Market

At one point, if you lived in Covington, Kentucky, and wanted to sell juggling supplies, you might find only a handful of people in your town who enjoyed juggling enough to purchase items from you.

However, with the Internet, you open up the world as your potential customer base. I use this obscure example of juggling because I know of a man who makes over $100,000 a year selling juggling supplies online.

There are forums where niche markets hang out, Facebook groups where they congregate, and blogs discussing their topic. It's your job to show up where they hang out, and it is easier than ever to do just that.

5. Automation

One of the things that I love about an online business is the fact that it can be automated. The business can run without you. Let me give you some examples:

You can automate the collecting of e-mail addresses from your prospects.

You can automate your follow-up e-mails that are sent to these prospects.

You can automate the purchasing of the products so people can order and receive their product while you're enjoying hanging out with your family.

6. You Can Run the Business from Anywhere in the World

With technology how it is today, you can be anywhere in the world and still run your business. Especially with the use of smartphones. You can answer e-mails from customers, hire help, and even run your marketing right from your smartphone now.

7. Outsource Help

I mentioned above that when you start an online business, you open it up to the world. I'm not referring to just customers either. I'm also talking about help. You now have access to qualified people from all around the world who can help you run your business.

Here are five places that you can find great help:
- Fiverr.com
- oDesk.com
- Freelancer.com
- Scriptlance.com
- Craigslist.org

There you have it. Seven good (even great) reasons why an online business makes perfect sense. If these reasons don't fire you up with excitement, then I don't know what will.

2

---

8 Red Hot Ways You Can Start Making Money Online

The dream . . .

Finding the perfect online business, working in your pajamas at home while drinking coffee, and making enough money to pay all your bills and then some.

Sounds too good to be true, right? I'm here to tell you that there are people from all walks of life who are doing this every day. In fact, in this book, I share several of their stories.

There are plenty of ways to make money online. Some you might pass on, while others might cause you to perk up. I have compiled eight red hot ways that you can legitimately make money online.

1. Blogging

If, while reading this, you're thinking to yourself, "Man, I could write this myself," then maybe blogging is opportunity that might be right for you. Blogging is ideal for those who have a hobby they love or who are obsessed about a particular topic, and have the ability to take their love for that topic and put it down in writing.

Now, obviously, the idea is not just to write a blog as if it was your diary. You're writing because you want to get paid. How you do this? There are many ways to get paid as a blogger. Here are a few ways:

- Selling advertising
- Using Google AdSense
- Selling links to websites from your blog
- Promoting affiliate products
- Creating and selling your own products
- Selling a service

Some individuals who have successful blogs have been able to quit their day jobs entirely, and they are able to focus all their attention on blogging while living off the money they make from advertising or selling products online.

2. Become a Freelancer

If you have a service that you can deliver to others all across the world, setting up an online business to do so is a great way to make money fast. In fact, it's one of the fastest ways to be in business with very little cost. It's simply providing a service and getting paid once it is delivered. That simple.

3. Become a Call Center Rep

Every business out there has a customer service department. Basically, what this boils down to is a group of people who are either answering phones or sending e-mails in response to customer complaints or questions. More and more, businesses are looking for individuals who work from home to perform these customer service jobs. Really, all a person needs to have in their home in order to do this is a steady Internet connection, and, at times, a landline telephone. Now, these jobs are not going to make you a millionaire overnight; however, they can be a good way for an individual to have a steady income.

4. Selling Items on eBay.com and Amazon.com

By now, just about everybody has heard about eBay.com and Amazon.com. Many have thought about making money by selling items on these sites. However, they may be reluctant to do so, thinking that the eBay market is already saturated, and there's no way for them to make money. This is not necessarily the case.

It is true that it's not as easy to make money on eBay as it was when it first started. There are a lot of people doing it, and there are a lot of products for sale. The same principle applies to Amazon.com. However, if individuals go to work, build a good reputation, and set up display pages that are going to attract the attention of customers, both sites still offer an excellent way to make money from home.

5. Answer People's Questions

There are times when the information that is provided on search engines is not enough to answer questions that people have. So when they need a personalized answer, and they need it now, they turn to specialists to answer their questions. If a person is an expert in a particular field, this can be an effective way to make side money. Sites like Live Person, WebAnswers.com, and Just Answers are examples of sites that pay people to answer questions.

6. Affiliate Marketing

Sites like Amazon.com offer commissions of up to 25% to individuals who will promote the products they have for sale. Anytime someone purchases a product that you promote, you get a cut. And you have the opportunity to choose from millions of products. There are several sites that list companies that have products for sale and will pay you a commission for either a lead or a sale.

What's great about affiliate marketing is that you can write a blog post reviewing a product that you believe in and insert your affiliate links in the post. Therefore, if someone wants to purchase it (even in the middle of the night), you will make money. This could go on for years!

7. Membership Sites

From a website that assists children's book authors write and promote their books to a website that charges a monthly fee to have weekly meals sent to members, the types of membership sites out there on the web are endless.

8. Informational Products

Creating your own informational products can be a great way to create passive income for yourself online. The key is finding a problem that people are willing to pay money to solve. The top three biggest niches are health, wealth, and relationships.

Your informational product could be a downloadable e-book or a printed newsletter that you send out each month to paying customers. There are many different options from which you can choose.

3

Top 6 Fatal Mistakes Online Newbies Make and How to Avoid Them

While learning all the latest and greatest tips for making money online can be profitable, so is avoiding the deadly mistakes that newbies make when they first start an online business. These tips can save you a lot of time, energy, and resources for sure.

Picture for a moment what it would be like if you could move right to the head of the class because you're avoiding the most common mistakes? Imagine how you would feel if you knew you could get to making money a lot quicker.

The good news is that dreaming about avoiding the most common problems isn't just a fantasy—it CAN happen. Below you'll find the top six mistakes that I see people make regularly and how to avoid them in your own business.

1. They treat their business like a hobby and not a business.

One of the awesome things about an online business is the fact that it doesn't take much money to get started. The bad thing about an online business is the fact that it doesn't take much money to get started.

Sometimes when we don't have much invested in something, it can be very easy to start coming up with excuses not to do what we need to do. For instance, you might have working hours scheduled to work on certain areas of your business. However, with nobody holding you accountable, it's very easy to slack off instead of working on your income-producing activity as you had scheduled.

When you start an online business, treat it like you just spent $100,000 on it. If you do that, then you're more likely to follow through with your activities.

2. They try to do too many businesses or programs at once.

Information, information, information!

It's everywhere. That's a positive and a negative. We'll discuss the negative in this case.

Many times, I see a newbie join a program or start a new online business and then thirty to ninety days later, they're doing something else on top of their original commitment. The problem with that is that now they're having to build traffic, build an e-mail list, and craft offers for an entire new website. That becomes draining very quickly, and then both projects tend to fail.

It's very important to commit to your business for a certain amount of time. I suggest twelve months. It takes time to build a business. There's no way around it.

3. They don't choose the right business for them.

There are a million ways to make money online (well, maybe not millions), and sometimes a person who is anxious to get started will jump into a business that isn't the right fit for them. They may see dollar signs, but deep down they have very little desire for the business. Other times a friend may put pressure on the person to join a network marketing program with them and, again, the true desire for the business isn't there in the first place.

The key is to be honest with yourself about who you are and what you want to do with your working hours. Take some time and decide what type of business you want and what you're willing to do to make that happen. Ask your friends about what strengths they see in you. Doing this exercise will help you avoid choosing the wrong business for you.

4. They don't build a list.

This is a big one. I have seen online entrepreneurs lose their businesses because a traffic source dried up and they never built an e-mail database to market back to (when they have something to sell). If they did have a database they could go back to, then they could simply send out their offers and be back in the game.

When you start your business, start offering something for free in exchange for a prospect's contact information. Think about what you can give away that will get your prospects excited. Once you have a database, begin to send out interesting e-mails that include both great content and great offers.

5. They don't have a USP.

USP stands for "unique selling proposition." It's what makes you stand out in the sea of competition. Ask yourself what it is that makes you different from everyone else in the marketplace. Many online entrepreneurs have never asked themselves this, and they end up looking just like everyone else in the marketplace.

List all the reasons why someone should do business with you, and then start using that information in all your marketing and branding.

6. They don't survey their prospects and customers.

The more you know about someone's wants and desires, the better your sales message will become. One of the best ways to learn more about your target market is to survey them; however, many newbies fail to do this.

One of my marketing friends sent a survey to his list a few years back and then took the data and updated his homepage. Instantly, he started receiving more e-mail addresses from his prospects and his income went up. It didn't cost him any more money to do this either.

Here are some questions you might ask on a survey:
- Sex
- Age
- Location
- How they found your website
- Top questions they have about a topic
- What other websites they visit about a certain topic
- What their goals are

These are just a few examples of what you could ask a prospect/customer that could help you determine what marketing is working or why they decided to buy from you. Both are very important pieces of information.

You have just learned six of the top fatal mistakes that newbie on-line marketers make. Hopefully you will take this knowledge to heart and not make the same mistakes. By doing so, you're guaranteed to reach your goals much faster.

4

4 Powerful Ways to Drive Massive Amounts of Traffic to Your Website

An effective website marketing strategy can increase client loyalty, improve an online search engine ranking, increase traffic to a website, and improve online credibility. The Internet is a hub of online activity. A website with an effective online presence can reach new clients and build a solid reputation. There are several ways to drive massive amounts of traffic to your website. Viral marketing, SEO (Search Engine Optimization) marketing, and comprehensive market research are profitable advertising strategies for generating large amounts of online traffic.

1. Using viral marketing and social media can drive massive amounts of traffic to your website.

Viral marketing refers to certain marketing techniques that use social networks and other electronic methods to provide exponential product exposure and product brand recognition. These viral marketing methods can be self-replicating and produce a virus-like expansion for a product or service on the Internet. There are various types of viral marketing campaigns that may be used to generate large amounts of traffic for a website customer. These marketing campaigns may include the following:

A pass message encourages one user to pass the message on to other users. Social media sites often use this style of chain-mail marketing. Circulation may occur through Facebook entries or online videos. Word of mouth is often used to circulate a particular product message.

A viral-encouraged reward may be used in order to generate client loyalty, for example. An e-mail can be sent from one person and forwarded on to another. A third party may be required to do something. Online contests are used in this format, and a chance to win is provided by a third party.

Undercover marketing is a viral message presented as a page and includes attractive or unusual news. Undercover marketing is not immediately apparent.

Fan clubs or associations of friends may create an environment that is typical for a fan club group. This method of product advertising uses online forums and blogging to discuss certain developments of a company or product, for example.

2. Using SEO and online marketing can double sales leads for your website.

SEO and online marketing are types of product exposure that use link building and social SEO applications. Getting the best value from online marketing may include certain tactics, and these tactics are the following:

- SEO and online marketing are link building. A product issue may need to be irritated and a solution provided.
- SEO marketing may include certain structured Internet programming techniques. These electronic methods involve keyword research and building an online presence with the various search engines.
- Keyword searches are important for any high-return activity on the modern Internet. Terms and phrases are used to target certain consumer needs.
- Keyword searches can be used to change market conditions and understand the motivations of consumers in certain product niches.

3. Using market research and e-mail marketing will outshine your competition.

This style of online advertising can produce a massive amount of traffic for a website presence. There are certain requirements of effective market research that need to be included with any online marketing plan.

Market research usually includes a comprehensive analysis of the branding process, the online competition, and the selected product strategy.

Branding creates a successful return on investment. Branding produces a certain ranking within a niche market. The strengths and weaknesses of a product or service can differentiate a particular company from the rest of the competition. A brand is the name or symbol and other features that identify a seller's goods and services. An image will sell a product over a competitor's, for example. A logo is a company personality and identity. Customers see an intrinsic value attached to a brand's value. A product or service logo has its own company equity, and this image equity accompanies the business name.

A brand image may be used successfully to set a business or product apart from its competition. Customers who purchase a particular product are using a brand experience in order to select the best product for themselves.

Brand awareness refers to a customer's ability to recall and recognize a product under different market conditions. Branding can be accomplished by a company through the use of business names or logos, for example. A jingle can be used as a branding technique as well.

Brands may be made up of a name, logo, and tag line. Graphics are often used to provide successful product awareness for a general consumer audience. Shapes and product colors are important elements used in a product branding.

Competitor analysis is an important part of any successful marketing campaign on the Internet. Competitor analysis uses trends and day-to-day information that impacts a general buying audience. Industry reports are important to analyze.

A successful product strategy needs to be selected. A product strategy offers solutions for at least six months out into the product's future. A product strategy will include predictions and plans for a business.

Market research involves the strengths and weaknesses of a company and its products. A marketing plan identifies successful opportunities within a niche market, for example. A plan will help a business connect the dots and confidently move a business into a successful future.

E-mail marketing is a successful and modern method of attracting certain niche market customers. This style of online advertising mostly involves direct e-mails to previous customers. Direct e-mails can include promotional and special offers.

E-mail marketing has its advantages for a new business online. E-mail advertising offers a tracking system and can include a direct customer response service. This style of advertising is less expensive and faster than traditional mail, for example.

Transactional e-mail marketing is usually triggered based on a customer's action. Transactional e-mails may be generated through dropped-basket messages, a purchase, or an order confirmation. E-mail receipts can generate transactional e-mails with a company, for example.

4. Using on-page marketing can successfully affect your search engine rankings.

On-page marketing includes the effective website development of a company's Internet business. A successful website is one that has several on-page factors.

On-page factors are required in order for a company's Internet website to be effective and profitable. On-page factors include the general content of the website page, which needs to be worthy of a search engine result position. The user is looking for a certain product or service, and a worthy web page is one that delivers this type of consumer result.

A search engine will read and crawl over a web page, searching for certain information that a consumer is looking for online. Good content is necessary for a web page and should have the content that the consumer is demanding. The web page is linkable if the content is good.

Online customers need to be able to link to a web page. Search engines are more likely to rank a web page higher if a general consumer audience is able to link to a certain product or service on a web page.

A title tag is the second most important factor for a page to have. SEO advertising uses a title tag to generate traffic for a company website, for example.

The website URL is important. The SEO categories chosen for a website URL are critical for some types of online advertising. A URL shows the hierarchy of the information on a page, for example. This information is used by Internet search engines to determine the relevancy of the given web page for an online marketing audience.

Images used along with text on a page are frequently used to enhance the marketing value of page content. Images are easy to find and tend to generate a positive audience response for a product or service.

The website needs to be SEO friendly with valuable content. The content needs to be indexed effectively. Information display methods for an online presence are frequently used to generate audience interest and attraction.

There are several methods that may be used to generate profitable traffic to a website. Viral marketing methods are those that often use social media as an effective advertising platform for a ready-made audience. SEO advertising strategies are frequently used to double sales leads for an online company. Sales leads are produced using keyword values that are carefully researched for a company. On-page website design and effective e-mail advertising can successfully generate needed business profits.

5

Deborah's Hot List— 12 Resources Every Online Entrepreneur Ought to Use

When you're starting out online, it's very easy to get overwhelmed and not know which resources are helpful and which resources you should run from. Below are ten resources that I highly recommend to others starting out. They are the same resources that I am using in my own business.

1. www.FollowDeborah.com/aweber—If you're going to have an online business, then you're going to need an autoresponder. I use AWeber to follow up automatically with all my leads, and I use it to send messages to thousands of prospects all at once. Your list is like gold to your online business.

2. www.FollowDeborah.com/master-resale-rights—Here you can find low-cost products that you can give away as a bonus offer. If you're going to make an offer to your list, you'll want to offer your prospects some bonuses. Remember, you're in competition with others who are trying to get the same customers, so be sure to offer bonuses that will attract customers to your offer. An added bonus is that you can also use these products yourself!

3. www.FollowDeborah.com/leadpages—One of the first things you'll want to do when you start your online business is find leads. Here you can find done-for-you sales pages, webinar pages, bonus pages. This will save you so much time, and your time is one of the most valuable assets you have in your business!

4. www.FollowDeborah.com/hostgator—Need hosting for your website? I find Hostgator to provide awesome customer service, and their hosting service is easy to follow and understand.

5. www.FollowDeborah.com/godaddy—I like to get all my domains in one place. I just find they're easier to keep up with that way, and you can find any domain you'll ever need here.

6. *www.FollowDeborah.com/TopTierBiz*—If you're looking for a top-tier online business, you'll definitely want to check out MOBE. "Top tier" simply means the products are high end and you can make commissions upward of $5,000. The best thing about top-tier business is that the phone team will sell these products for you and you'll make the commission.

7. *www.FollowDeborah.com/Rmm-video*—If you're already stretched for time and you're looking for a passive income stream with an online business, then I highly recommend checking out this website.

8. *www.FollowDeborah.com/stayconnected*—It doesn't matter if you have an online business or an offline business, the most important aspect of any business is staying connected with your prospects and customers and letting them know how important they are to you. This tool gives you everything you need to stay connected in a personal way.

9. *www.FollowDeborah.com/getanswers*—If you're looking for "something," but just don't really know what's best for you. Do you have questions but don't know where to find the answers. The solution is to schedule a free thirty-minute "get answers" session here.

10. *www.FollowDeborah.com/guide*—Get this no-nonsense guide. The exact business model that a seven-figure Internet marketer used to go from making $700/month to making $314,900.29/month is described in this guide. This guide will show you what an online "franchise" model looks like.

11. *www.FollowDeborah.com/21steps*—I love to learn by following simple steps that put everything in the right order. These twenty-one steps are easy to follow, and most can be completed within thirty minutes. PLUS, you get a personal coach, a six-figure earner, to guide you along the way.

12. *www.FollowDeborah.com/create*—You can go here and learn to create your own informational product where you can keep 100% of the profit. You'll actually watch as an informational product is created. Just follow the steps and create your own.

6

12 Real-World Case Studies of Successful Online Entrepreneurs

When I first started online, I wasn't all that confident that online marketing could work for me. One of the things that helped me overcome that limiting belief was hearing the stories of people just like me who had found success online with various businesses.

There's no shortage of stories of people who have taken the plunge and ventured out on their own to make money. In this chapter, you'll read some interviews that I conducted with several highly successful online entrepreneurs.

I hope these interviews inspire you to action and start you on the path to creating your own success story.

Name: Helen Avery

Where are you from?

I was born in Longmont, Colorado, born and raised, but we moved to Newberg, Oregon, in 2009.

Former career (or present career if still working):

Former career was a general manager in a restaurant. Now I am an online marketer, speaker, and personal development coach.

Can you tell us a little bit about how you make money online?

I coach clients on how to build their marketing funnels, I create products that help others achieve their online goals, and I market affiliate products' online websites.

How did you get started in an online business?

I actually was trying to get a website built to market my husband's pencil art at www.marks-drawing-portraits.com. We struggled trying to figure out how to fit all the puzzle pieces together. But as we did it, I started to realize the potential I had to do greater things with my knowledge and figured out how to help others by sharing that with them.

When did you first decide that an online business was right for you?

I wrote the e-mail below and it actually tells a little bit of that story, so here is a copy of that e-mail because it was this defining moment, when I look back, that made me decide being an online marketer and entrepreneur was meant to be:

"Giving Up is Not an Option" and "Everything Happens For a Reason"

I know it sounds cliché, but . . .

We are going to tell you our story over the next seven days. I hope you come along on this journey, because we really aren't that different than any of you out there who are searching for something better.

By the end of this series, you will completely know who Helen and

Mark are and maybe, just maybe, you will really understand what it means when I say "everything happens for a reason."

So here it goes!

Mark and I started on a journey in 2008 that really started us in a direction to finding a better lifestyle and wanting to find our passion in life. The questions that HAUNTED us were:

- What the heck was it supposed to be?
- What are we supposed to do?
- How are we supposed to even find it? and
- Where do you even look?

I found myself in my mid-thirties, wanting something more and not having a clue as to what that something was supposed to be. I had been very successful as a restaurant general manager, but my body was breaking down from the long hours of being on my feet all day. By 2006, I'd had a total of four surgeries on my feet, all for different things related to my running and being on my feet.

I was watching Mark struggling with his job as a cultured stone salesman (you know, the fake stone you see on the fronts of buildings and houses or on fireplaces) and coming home from work each night completely unhappy and complaining of . . .

- the stress;
- his boss;
- the hours he had to work;
- the pressure;
- and the list goes on.

Oh yeah, and did I say the PRESSURE? It was like it was leaking the life right out of his face.

If only I could describe the look on his face when he came home that night. He'd lost a $45,000 sale, or some other ungodly amount of money, to another company that underbid his offer—all to put some rocks on the front of a new hotel that was being built.

It's hard watching the person you love fall apart because the next day he would have to tell his boss that they lost the bid.

He was in fear of telling his boss the news. He was under stress to make the sales (in a failing economy). He was scared to death he was going to lose his job. Most of all, I think he was just afraid of letting me down.

And then you get this sinking feeling in your stomach, that gut wrenching queasiness, that makes you want to puke and cry and just plain freak out over how you will pay the bills and next month's rent if you lose your job!

That day was the beginning for us. You will hear me say this a lot, "everything happens for a reason." That day happened for a reason, and the journey begins . . .

How long did it take you to get you to where you are now, and what would you say to our readers who are just getting started?

Well, that day was in July 2008, and each and every day since then has been a step forward in that journey. It has taken a true inner desire for me personally to find true purpose in giving to others.

You see, this isn't about making money online and finding a new career; it's about truly awakening to a consciousness different from the way I was brought up and being able to give back to others in a way that gives them the results they are looking for.

If you can actually detach from actually making money and know that the actions you take are of a giving nature and a showing of your true authentic self, the results you can achieve are limitless.

What are the top three to five areas readers should concentrate on when starting off?

Personal development, or your mindset. It's easy to say you want to go out and do something like this, but probably 95% of the time, people quit because they have too many limiting beliefs. You need to invest in yourself.

Pick one thing you are passionate about and go with it. Jumping from program to program will stop you in your tracks, and you'll never get anywhere. Information overload sets in and then you can easily sink yourself.

Do your research and invest in coaching. Having a coach was vital for my success. You need to educate yourself and have guidance. Having someone to help you keep on track is extremely important.

Network with like-minded people. Join groups, clubs, or master-minds, and surround yourself with people who will propel you to the next level. Ask yourself—who do you hang out with now and how do they influence you? Do they bring you down, complain? Are always negative and never happy? If so, then you need to change the people you hang out with and get with positive, happy, outgoing entrepreneurs who can help lift your spirit and move forward.

Invest in yourself. There are no get-rich-overnight programs online. It takes hard work and dedication to learn how to produce results for yourself. You have to take appropriate actions to achieve the results you want. Sometimes it does mean investing in programs that will teach you and give you the tools and help you develop a mindset to do this on your own.

Can you recommend some quality resources for our readers, that have helped you? Here are some books and resources that I recommend:

- *The Power of Now*—Eckart Tolle
- *Inner Voice*—Russ Whitney
- *The Success Principles*—Jack Canfield
- *The 4-Hour Work Week*—Timothy Ferriss

www.theultimategameoflife.com
—The ninety-day challenge is life changing.
www.speakingempire.com
—If you want to propel yourself to a new level and speak on stage.

What's your favorite way to drive traffic to your website?

That's a hard question! You have to use a mixture of resources to get people to your site. SEO is key for my website, but in building my list I send clicks through solo ads, social media, YouTube videos, and ppc. They all kind of work in congruence with one another. Most importantly, I develop relationships with people and I'm not afraid to pick up the phone or chat with them live on Skype.

What are some pitfalls that our readers should be on the lookout for, and how can they be avoided?

Information overload and SOS (Shiny Object Syndrome). Quit buying every offer you see, thinking it's going to be the next best thing to make you money. It's not the products that do the work, it's you!

What's the biggest mistake you made getting started?

I didn't make any mistakes; I only failed to move forward fast. If anything, not believing I needed to invest more in myself and my mindset more than anything.

What big mistakes do you see others make?

Relying on products or programs, thinking they will do the work for them. People are looking for the easy road out, but they don't want to take the action to actually do it. Many times the actions they take are only running them in a cycle of insanity; instead of thinking about giving, they only look to get.

What information do you wish you'd had when you were first starting out?

My level of consciousness. I was thinking from my mind's perspective—or my ego's—and not really being truthful to myself or others. Once I woke up to that, everything changed.

What do you think are the keys to becoming a successful online?

ITAR:

Influence

Teaching

Actions

Results

It's an acronym for reaching the results you want by taking the actions to get yourself there while teaching and helping others and surrounding yourself with influential people.

If you take a simple approach and don't complicate things, you can obtain any success you want.

In your opinion, how can someone stand out among the competition?

Tell your story and be truly authentic. You just need to be you!

What are some things that you do NOT recommend for online entrepreneurs?

Spam your links to your friends! Tell me the program you bought today is gonna change your life and that I should buy it too.

Honestly (and I know a ton of marketers do this for social proof), I am against promoting my monetary gains to collect leads.

What's one of the things that you find most challenging about an online business?

The information and learning curve at the beginning is hard. Once you start to understand everything, then figuring out how to outsource it.

What's your favorite part of your day as an online marketer?

The fact that I choose my own schedule and that I can do it anywhere I have Internet access. Its freedom to know that money is coming to your bank account day and night without the worry of a JOB!

What does it really take to succeed in business, in your opinion?

Wake up! Tell your EGO to take a hike and give back. Do what you are passionate about and live your true life's purpose! It really does happen once you figure that out.

If you had to share three to five keys to building a successful online business, what would they be in order of priority?

- Mindset—Fix yours, because it's probably what's kept you where you're at right now. Get influenced by people who you want to be like and not by those who are where you have been stuck.
- Set goals—Have a plan and take action on your goals.
- Keep it simple—Do one thing, get good at it, and then move on.

For each of those keys, what are some goals that our readers should set for reaching each one of them?

- Read a motivational book, listen to blog talk radio, meditate daily, do what it takes to give your mind new programming each and every day with positive influence for your business desires.
- Take daily actions to move toward your goals. Look at the for-

ward progress you've made and not at all the reasons why you didn't get it done.
- Remember to breathe.
- Stay healthy in mind, body, and spirit.
- Set a healthy, wealthy, and happy goal to work toward.
- Pay attention to your environment—and if something isn't working, change it.
- Listen to your inner gut! That is where your truth lies!

What are some realistic long-term and short-term goals for our readers?

I can't tell you that because everyone is different. We all come from different upbringings, and we all have different life experiences.

All I do know is that each and every person has the potential inside to set a goal and achieve it if they truly want it! It's completely up to you.

What's the first thing you recommend our readers do after they're done reading this book?

Write down your wants. List the things you're passionate about. Ask yourself what your purpose is (the reason you're here on this earth), and make a plan to do something you're passionate about that will help your live out that purpose.

It will feel right and you will know it. Quit asking, "How do I make money at this?" and focus on what you love doing.

Who are the people that inspired you and why?

My daughter Chelsea. She came to me as a gift and as a reason for me to truly understand my purpose, to wake me up from a deep sleep and put me on a pathway to greatness.

Why?

Because it took me losing her to a drowning accident when she was thirteen months old to realize it. I saw what that little girl did for millions of people in a one-year timeframe and at the same time saw what she was doing for me and our family by making the sacrifice she did.

I have always said everything happens for a reason and I know she chose me to be her mother because I had the strength to carry on and do great things for others. It took her leaving me in the physical body to wake me up to how blindly I was going through life. Because of her, I now have a sense of peace and happiness I never knew possible and my life has purpose.

What did you learn from those people, that you'd like to pass on to our readers?

It's hard to convey what you go through when you lose a child, especially in the way we did. All I know is that every one of us has a soul and spirit inside, and, from the time we are born, we get shut down over and over again, being told how to do things by people who don't know any better themselves.

When you can shut off the voice in your head that keeps holding you back and listen to your heart and find that inner spirit that's just waiting to carry you, it's an amazing feeling. I just pray for people to not have to figure it out the way I did.

What tools/resources would you say are essential to doing marketing online?

www.infinitymarketingempire.com. We create results by building websites, coaching, and helping people get their passions working for them online.

What final words of wisdom would you like to pass on to everyone who's reading this chapter?

There is a reason why only 3% to 5% of people who try to do things online actually succeed. It takes a certain level of stubbornness, strong will, and determination, but mostly it needs to be an inner desire to want to help others.

When you find the happiness of giving, by doing things you love to do, you will change lives! When you do that, there's no better satisfaction—and the earth we live on, the air we breathe, and the energy among us grows stronger and creates an enlightened state of awareness. If I can do this after what I have gone through, then I know anyone can. Anything is possible if you just set your HEART to it!

Name: Andrea Goodsaid

Where are you from?

I grew up on the Upper West Side in New York City.

Former career (or present career if still working):

For years I was a craft show jeweler, the juried kind. I made and sold stained and fused glass jewelry that I made by hand. I had to leave the craft shows behind when my middle child was two because she was a social butterfly and wouldn't stay at our display. Then I started wholesaling and really had to work at producing day and night to make a living.

Can you tell us a little bit about how you make money online?

I make money online by serving my audience high-ticket affiliate programs (typically $1,000+ commissions per sale) that will help them by shortcutting their online journey and through coaching offers that I wrap around those transactions.

How did you get started in an online business?

I've been "online" since before the web—I remember dialing in to university bulletin boards. Then when the web became more viable, I used to participate in what were called "listservs"—essentially topic-based chat groups via e-mail. We thought it was so much fun to spam each other. Started tinkering right away at different make-money schemes.

When did you first decide that an online business was right for you?

In 2005, I decided that I needed to create a system that I could give away to people so they could also work online. I failed. The Internet had finally caught up to where you didn't have to be a super geek in order to take advantage of online tools, people were beginning to create systems for the masses, and Blogger and Wordpress were finally relatively user-friendly. In 2009, I finally decided that I had to make online income my only income.

How long did it take you to get you to where you are now, and what would you say to our readers who are just getting started?
Until 2012, my online work was still very labor intensive. I was still essentially trading time for money. In 2012, I switched over to large commissions and haven't looked back.

What are the top three to five areas readers should concentrate on when starting off?
- Mindset
- List building
- Irresistible offers

Can you recommend some quality resources for our readers, that have helped you?
Mark Hoverson's "Secret Beliefs" training
Dan Kennedy's books
The people you'll meet along the way

What's your favorite way to drive traffic to your website?
Webinars.

What are some pitfalls that our readers should be on the lookout for, and how can they be avoided?
They look for "traffic" instead of "audience"—"traffic" is lottery mentality . . . an "audience" you serve. An audience is what will make you wealthy. They buy new training because it feels good to buy it and then never open it. But often, strategically, they get one golden nugget from it and call it good enough.

Decide whether it'll serve your audience to buy it too and sell it to them if it will. They feel guilty about buying new training because they haven't finished the other stuff hanging around. Think of yourself as a curator—you don't have to know every dusty corner of a training, you just need to have the vision of how that one golden nugget will help your audience.

What's the biggest mistake you made getting started?
Going too far down the tech path. And not getting a mentor.

What big mistakes do you see others make?
Not asking for help. Having an "I need to know how to do everything and know it before I begin" frame of mind. Being a lone wolf. Collaboration, mentorship, and partnership are what it takes to make an online business work speedily.

What information do you wish you'd had when you were first starting out?
I wish I'd started building my list sooner. Your subscriber list is an asset forever when done correctly.

What do you think are the keys to becoming successful online?
Persistence. Willingness to fail and learn from it (reset your sails). And certainty that you can come out on the other end eventually.

In your opinion, how can someone stand out among the competition?
It's possible to "out consistent" most people. Get visible in lots of places via video, helping people in forums, getting on leaderboards, etc.

What are some things that you do NOT recommend for online entrepreneurs?
Forgetting that offline marketing exists too.

What's one of the things that you find most challenging about an online business?
Focusing on one project at a time (so I don't, lol).

What's your favorite part of your day as an online marketer?
The part where I'm doing something I want "just because I can." In other words, work can always bend to my LIFE schedule.

What does it really take to succeed in business, in your opinion?
A no-quit attitude.

If you had to share three to five keys to building a successful online business, what would they be in order of priority?

Commit to a lifetime of personal development.

Seek out like minds to network, brainstorm, and collaborate with.

Decide to lead.

For each of those three keys, what are some goals that our readers should set for reaching each one of them?

Daily reading/audio.

Get to events.

Notice places where you get stuck and become the solution.

What are some realistic long-term and short-term goals for our readers?

Totally depends on the person. The sky's literally the limit just as soon as you believe it to be possible for you.

What's the first thing you recommend our readers do after they're done reading this book?

Take action.

Who are the people that inspired you and why?

Mark Hoverson is probably my biggest inspiration source. He's the one who's caused me to take action in my business and embrace leadership.

What did you learn from those people, that you'd like to pass on to our readers?

Money loves speed.

What tools/resources would you say are essential to doing this?

It varies a little, depending on the type of marketing it is you want to be engaged in. Domains, hosting for opt-in pages, and a tool for collecting contact info into a database—bare minimum.

What final words of wisdom would you like to pass on to everyone who's reading this chapter?

Mindset is the key that can unlock any door you wish. Become a problem solver and a solutions provider. Serve your audience transformational transactions and you can only succeed.

Name: Carolina Millan

Where are you from?

I'm from Chile, South America. I live in a city called Viña del Mar.

Former career (or present career if still working):

I used to work in human resources as a recruiter. Then I started working as a headhunter independently. I studied business engineering in Valparaiso, in Chile.

Can you tell us a little bit about how you make money online?

I make money online in different ways: as a consultant in social media and digital marketing, as a coach, as an online teacher, and as an affiliate marketing with different companies.

How did you get started in an online business?

I got started back in 2008, when I realized that I didn't want to be an employee anymore, even though I'd only had a job for six months! It was my first and last job.

When did you first decide that an online business was right for you?

At the beginning, I wasn't sure it was for me, because I was buying course after course and not implementing anything. But it was in 2010 that I finally quit my job and started working as a social media consultant. I was really enjoying that because I had managed to brand myself as an expert.

How long did it take you to get you to where you are now, and what would you say to our readers who are just getting started?

Well, it took me four years to finally make money online. But once I made my first commission, it was downhill from there. I started using my results as social proof, and I started to teach others how to do it. One mistake I made was not to have the right mentor; I thought I could do everything on my own, but when you're on your own it's just harder and takes longer.

If you're just getting started, find a person or a group of people you want to be like, people you want to model. Your success will be your responsibility, but it's still important to choose the right people to be around and learn from. Success won't come overnight, so don't give up if you don't see results in your first couple of months.

What are the top three to five areas readers should concentrate on when starting off?

First of all, focus on branding yourself if you want long-term success. Second, learn how to get traffic—pick one source and master it. Become really good at it, so that you can teach it to others. And focus on adding value to people without necessarily wanting something in return. When you give people what they want, you will also get what you want. Finally, never get too emotionally attached to a prospect or a situation until it really brings you results. If you spend too much time trying to convince people and then they don't join you, you'll feel bad. Let them come to you. And if they take too long to decide, make sure you decide for them and disqualify them from your team.

Can you recommend some quality resources for our readers, that have helped you?

I like reading mashable.com to be up to date with the latest social media and technology trends. Also the socialmediaexaminer.com blog.

What's your favorite way to drive traffic to your website?

My favorites are YouTube and Facebook. I like creating valuable content, and when people like it, they go to my website to learn more and contact me. Facebook is a great way to network with people and so is Twitter.

What are some pitfalls that our readers should be on the lookout for, and how can they be avoided?

Running out of cash flow and chasing shiny objects. Try to focus on one thing at a time—then once you master it, move on to the next!

What's the biggest mistake you made getting started?

Being always in learning mode and feeling like I could never be ready to take action, that I still needed to learn more. It's best to take action as soon as possible, even if it's not perfect and even if you lose a little money.

What big mistakes do you see others make?

People think they have to go around convincing people that their business is good. People who go to social media platforms and start pitching and spamming others with their biz op are making a big mistake.

What information do you wish you'd had when you were first starting out?

I wish I had known more about traffic. It always seemed to me like it was very hard and scary. It turned out it wasn't!

What do you think are the keys to becoming successful online?

First, you need to detach from money. When you're too emotionally attached to money, it's hard for you to reinvest back into your business to scale up. That's something I am still struggling with, but once you start caring less about money and more about helping people, money will come to you. Always serve others.

In your opinion, how can someone stand out among the competition?

By being themselves. Everyone is unique, and that's the main thing you need to show people—your uniqueness, there is no other you. Let people be attracted by your honesty, transparency, and leadership. Create content that people love and keep them coming back for more.

What are some things that you do NOT recommend for online entrepreneurs?

I don't recommend getting caught up with technical stuff. Try to outsource the things you cannot do and focus on the moneymaking activities: writing e-mails, talking to prospects on the phone, sending traffic, writing on your blog, making a video.

What's one of the things that you find most challenging about an online business?

Time management. It's hard to manage your time effectively, and sometimes you end up overworking yourself! Always try to find time for yourself. And, if you can, have an office outside your home.

What's your favorite part of your day as an online marketer?

Helping people and getting positive feedback from them! When they're either loving the training they're going through, or when they get their first sale!

What does it really take to succeed in business, in your opinion?

Perseverance is key. I've seen people quit after just one month. They don't take their business seriously enough and think results have to be fast. It's not always the case. Be patient, and always move forward.

If you had to share three to five keys to building a successful online business, what would they be in order of priority?

- Build your brand.
- Build relationships with people.
- Help people and teach them what they need to do step by step.

For each of those three keys, what are some goals that our readers should set for reaching each one of them?

Create your blog and social media profiles and do videos. Talk to people on the phone or Skype or meet them if you can. Create a system that allows you to automate part of the training you have for your team.

What are some realistic long-term and short-term goals for our readers?

Give your business at least six months. Results may definitely come sooner. Don't expect to reach five or six figures right away, go step by step—first your first $100, then $1,000, and then $10,000.

What's the first thing you recommend our readers do after they're done reading this book?

If you don't have a business you're working on yet, find one that you feel comfortable promoting. Also find a mentor that can help you take the first steps. And definitely, go out there and create your social media profiles on Facebook, Twitter, and YouTube, and start creating content!

Who are the people that inspired you and why?

Jonathan Budd, Mike Dillard, and Mark Hoverson—they're my favorite IM gurus.

What did you learn from those people, that you'd like to pass on to our readers?

Jonathan inspires me to be a better person and to have a better relationship with money and with life. Mike Dillard taught me everything I know about attraction marketing and nowadays I can say it's real! It happens to you! Mark Hoverson has a great style of teaching and telling stories, and I love that.

What tools/resources would you say are essential to doing this?

Get tools like Jing or Camtasia to create videos from your screen where you show your prospects and team members step-by-step instructions on how to start doing their marketing. Create a fan page on Facebook and post content daily, either your own or other people's. And make sure you have a camera to make good videos. An iPhone 5 camera is an excellent one you can use, so don't stress about having to buy an expensive one!

What final words of wisdom would you like to pass on to everyone who's reading this chapter?

Once you've read this book, go out there and implement what you've read. Don't be in a constant learning mode. It's important that you always improve your skills and acquire new ones by learning from others, but don't get stuck there. You'll be overwhelmed. Find something you can implement today and DO IT!

Name: Rob Paris

Where are you from?
Sweden.

Former career (or present career if still working):
Musician.

Can you tell us a little bit about how you make money online?
I drive traffic to my squeeze pages through different ways, like media buying, solo ads, banner ads, Facebook, etc. So I target traffic to my pages and get people to sign up to my list and then I provide them with value and great offers a couple of days a week. The thing about building a list with people interested in what you have to offer is that you can promote to them over and over again and always bring in sales.

The important thing is to build a relationship with your list so that they know you bring value and trust you, so they don't see your e-mails as spam. And as soon as someone buys something I have promoted to them, I follow up with them and make sure that they get the help they need and make sure they get results with the product they've invested in, especially MOBE products.

So what I do to make money online is to help others make money online. It's pretty funny, but that is how it works. What I mainly promote is funnels with high-ticket back-end products because that's the way to get really high commissions.

How did you get started in an online business?
It all started for me when I was a part of a personal development community and I saw an ad on that page—something like "make money online," very basic—but I clicked the ad and was taken to a sales page for a book about affiliate marketing. This was about 2007/2008. At

the time, I had no idea what affiliate marketing or internet marketing was at all, but as I was looking into it, I found it was really smart. I liked the idea of building my online business from home. I thought that I would make millions of dollars very fast, because that's how they marketed it back then—not so much anymore. I was buying product after product, learning and learning, and decided to start promoting "Learn Guitar" products since I've been a guitarist for about twenty years.

I started to record my guitar tutorial videos, struggled with all the tech stuff, all from setting up a page to putting together videos in a nice way and putting them online and on my page.

In the guitar niche, I made a few sales, but YouTube was filled with guitar tutorials and people don't want to pay like $47 for a membership, even though they would learn much faster that way.

So I understood I had to change niches. I decided to go with the online niche I loved the most, which was the "personal development, self-growth" niche, all about how to improve yourself and live a good life. So I actually wrote my book, struggling with it for a long time because of both the language barrier (I wrote it in English) and how I had to put it on Clickbank and create the whole sales funnel myself—everything from a free gift with a follow-up and the sales letter for the book, and bonuses to increase values, etc.

When I was done, I started to send some traffic and got a few sales, but because I only charged $29.95 for it, I very soon understood that I needed to have an upsell. I can tell you that upsell never came, it's still in progress. I don't know if I ever will get it done because I found a business that had ALL this done for me, everything from a free gift, to a front-end product, to a high-ticket back-end sales funnel, e-mail follow-up, etc.

So I was like, "What the heck, maybe it's better to do what's proven to work already, instead of trying to do it ALL myself," so I did, because I saw the potential and saw the quality of it. And about six months after starting promoting this new business, I found I had made close to $100,000 and a free Mercedes and it completely changed my and my family's life.

When did you first decide that an online business was right for you?

As I said above, when I first saw the information online that it was possible to make money online, I knew instantly that this was for me! I knew I would do it and make it happen. I am the kind of guy that NEVER gives up if there's something I want.

I struggled online for almost five years or so before I cracked my own code and found the right business, but now it's so worth it. I learned a lot during those years of struggle, about Internet marketing, and most importantly, about myself! I had to go through all this pain of not succeeding and all those hours in front of the computer and people thought I was insane, but I mean, take a look at me now, look who's talking! Haha.

How long did it take you to get you to where you are now, and what would you say to our readers who are just getting started?

Again, it took me five years, but if I'd known back then what I know now, it would go super fast. You don't need to do all the things I did, like trying to do it all yourself and creating your own products, etc. You just have to find a business that is proven to work where you can see others who are just like you getting good results. Then you can just follow that system and off you go, really. It doesn't have to be a long struggle. Having a STRONG WHY so you know why you are doing your business will help you never give up. You see, I have NEVER in my whole life seen anyone fail; I have only seen people QUIT! So, never quit and never give up your dream!

What are the top three to five areas readers should concentrate on when starting off?

Learn how to drive targeted traffic, build your list and build a relationship with that list. Find a high-converting offer with a high-ticket back-end, and promote that offer to your list giving them value and help. Also, take really good care of your buyers is my best tip. People buy high-ticket items if they feel safe doing it, and if you are there all the time helping out and so on, you'll end up making a lot of money.

So main focus:

HELP OTHERS! And the money will follow, trust me! When I changed focus from trying to make money to helping others, that's when the money came, and it came fast.

What's your favorite way to drive traffic to your website?
Media buying; banner ads, etc.; and solo ads.

What are some pitfalls that our readers should be on the lookout for, and how can they be avoided?
First thing is thinking that it will go really, really fast and it will be for free. The reality is that it doesn't look like that. If you want to start a real business, online or offline, it will require time and money; however, online Internet marketing is the best way to do it if you want to make money. That's because it's mostly digital products so the profit margin is really high. With that said, just do it. Create a simple page and drive traffic to it. Don't try to get it all perfect before you just start. It took me months and months to let that go. I was afraid it would not work—but a bad page does better than no page any day of the week. So just do it!

What's the biggest mistake you made getting started?
Tried to do it all myself, everything from sales letters, to products creation, to follow-up, etc. Plus, trying to make everything perfect.

What big mistakes do you see others make?
Focusing on getting free traffic and wanting to get everything for free. Also trying to get everything perfect before getting started. I see people who are too afraid of investing in themselves and their own businesses. Too many people are missing out on the money that they could be earning because they quit too soon or don't take responsibility for their business. Also, too many people are thinking too small. They don't think it's possible to make hundreds of thousands of dollars online.

What information do you wish you'd had when you were first starting out?
That I should do paid advertising and that I should license a product instead of just promoting products as an affiliate.

What do you think are the keys to becoming a successful online?
To see it as a real business and act as if it's impossible to fail! Never give up and believe in yourself. Persistence!

In your opinion, how can someone stand out among the competition?

Be yourself, make sure to do all you can to help other people, don't try to fit in and look and sound like other marketers, and work harder than anyone else!

What are some things that you do NOT recommend for online entrepreneurs?

To be "hypey" or talk about results you don't have yourself, like saying things like, "How I made $100k in six months" and yet you didn't do it. Stay true to yourself and others. Before you have your own results, market others' results or just show facts!

What's one of the things that you find most challenging about an online business?

Staying focused and making sure the time spent behind the computer is productive. Like right now, this is the first thing I am writing in the morning, before checking any e-mail or checking any stats from yesterday. Always make sure to do things that will have a big impact or income on your business before checking e-mail, etc.

You should make a list the day before on your three most income-producing activities and your three most impacting activities. Then, you should, if it does not require you to go to your inbox, do them before you do anything else. Don't clutter your brain with e-mails and Facebook before doing things that are important. Be productive, not just "busy."

Commitment and persistence! There will be some tough days. If you just know that, you'll get through it and the rewards are more than awesome! As with all the things you want to succeed in, you need commitment and you also need to feel it's fun to do it. You need a big WHY. Make sure to know WHY you are doing this! What is it you will do with the money you will earn, etc.

Also, another challenge is to keep to that throughout the day or the time you have set to work on your business. Don't check your e-mail or Facebook during that time. If you are waiting for answers, etc., check for that e-mail only and ignore the rest, then set aside time to go through your e-mail once or twice a day. UNSUBSCRIBE from most newsletters; you don't have time to go through all that information and still get things done.

What's your favorite part of your day as an online marketer?

Getting "thank you" e-mails! To see my students and team get results and have them thank me for it. I mean, to get a "thank you" from someone who just invested a large amount of money in a business, for example, means a lot to me. It means I have made them understand what this is all about and they are thanking me for showing them the business/product and also helping them out with their challenges. I love helping people out and getting them unstuck, etc.

If you had to share three to five keys to building a successful online business, what would they be in order of priority?

Treat it like a real business—It is a real business you are building here. If you're treating it as a hobby or an "I will try this out" kind of thing, your results will reflect that!

Take 100% responsibility for yourself and your results! Don't blame "him" or "her" or "nobody" if you don't get the results you want. It just means you have to change something and improve yourself and your process and system. Self-discipline! Never, never, ever give up!

Learn to earn—If you master traffic generation, learn to generate targeted traffic, and drive that traffic to a high-converting offer, you will ALWAYS be in profit! Also accept that this is a never-ending process.

Have the focus on helping others. If you shift your mindset from "I want to make money" to "How can I help others to make money?", you will succeed. Take the focus from yourself and put it on other people. I didn't believe that from the start, but as soon as I shifted— boom, money followed!

Be prepared to invest time and money in your business and then do it.

For each of those five keys, what are some goals that our readers should set for reaching each one of them?

Read and learn about what a real business looks like. The fundamentals of running an online business don't differ from running an offline business like a restaurant or a shoe store or even a rock band.

Every time you catch yourself blaming someone else for your results, make a reality check, slap your face, and tell yourself to stop wasting your time on blaming others for your results.

Don't give your power to someone else. You just have to change something that will change your results.

Decide on what traffic method you would like to master, and dig into it and master it—just one method, don't try to learn three, four, or five at once. You'll just be overwhelmed and slow down your process. Pick one and master it, that's it!

In the next month, help at least one other person to make a commission online—it's okay if it's just $25, just make sure to help someone else make money. Trust me, it's important, and an awesome feeling!

Set a dollar amount that you want to invest in your business and go and invest with it right away. It might be a traffic course, or it might be to outscore a creation of a lead magnet you can use to capture your own leads, or it might be an investment in paid traffic to an affiliate offer, but just do it now. You will have to invest money to grow your business, so you should start right away.

What are some realistic long-term and short-term goals for our readers?

Short-term: Set a goal to help at least ten other people to get results with the product(s) you are promoting. That is much more than most people ever do. If you never made a sale/commission online, set a goal to make your first sale within thirty days and do whatever it takes to make it! Start today, right now, today!

Long-term: Live on it! Make so much money that you don't need to do anything else to generate money. That's super realistic, but it will require time and money to get there—that's it!

What's the first thing you recommend our readers do after they're done reading this book?

If I was brand new, I would simplify the process and do this: Do some research to find a high-converting offer and then drive traffic to it using solo ads. That's it. So you can get a feel of what it's all about. Don't get in the tech part if you don't like it or don't know anything about it. Just drive traffic to the links—you'll get to promote the product and get some sales.

After you've done this for a little while, you'll want to get your own squeeze page so you can drive traffic to that one and build your list. When you do that, you'll be able to e-mail that list with content whenever you want to—both helpful stuff but also offers you can make money on.

Who are the people that inspired you and why?

In the Internet-marketing area, Eban Pagan, Frank Kern, Jonathan Budd, and also Matt Lloyd, among many others.

What did you learn from those people, that you'd like to pass on to our readers?

What I have written about above.

What tools/resources would you say are essential to doing IM?

An autoresponder like AWeber to build your list of leads and customers!

What final words of wisdom would you like to pass on to everyone who's reading this chapter?

If I can do it, YOU can do it! I started with nothing, worked my way up. Keep it simple, have self-discipline, work on your business six days a week. Believe in yourself. The business is proven to work, so you just need to do it. And, you know, don't listen to what the naysayers say like, "That's not possible," or "You can't make money online, it's just a myth," or whatever, because "those that say it can't be done should get out of the way of those doing it."

Name: Robert Tepper

Where are you from?

I grew up in Northwest Baltimore, in Randallstown, Maryland. I was my high school valedictorian, with just over five hundred in the class. I went to college at Duke in North Carolina, then to graduate school at Stanford in California, and had my first post-university job in Allentown, Pennsylvania. I moved to San Diego in 1984 and I have never looked back.

Former career (or present career if still working):

Electrical engineer, serial entrepreneur, and educator. My first job was with AT&T Bell Laboratories in Allentown, Pennsylvania. They paid my way through graduate school at Stanford University through their "One Year on Campus" or "OYOC" program. My final quarter at Stanford was the best. I was done with all my tough classes and really able to appreciate what campus life had to offer. I swam and played tennis just about every day and was social chairman of my dorm, which was filled with international students for the summer quarter.

I worked for AMCC for fifteen years, first as a design engineer and then a design manager, and then had several other management roles. One of the perks that attracted me to AMCC in 1984 was a very generous stock option plan. The company had plans for an IPO from the day I joined; that was a big factor in my decision to join the company. After preparing twice for an IPO and twice pulling back due to market conditions throughout the fifteen years, I was always doing startups on the side. I developed business plans for everything from a for-profit curbside recycling program, to an international travel consolidator, to a home automation products company, among others, prior to getting married.

Post marriage, for several years, my Brazilian wife and I had a business working with Xerox laser printers in the Brazilian market. While that was an exciting business and made good profits for those in Brazil who were running the day-to-day operations, it never produced a profit for my wife and me. Nonetheless, I continually invested in one business or another, knowing that any success requires time testing and optimization, and that success is the result of having failed enough times.

By 1997, I was divorced and paying alimony and child support, including private school tuition for my kids, with money I didn't have. In spite of making good money as an engineer, it was not enough to cover the costs of raising a family and investing in a business with money left over.

AMCC finally went public in 1997. The stock came out at $8.50 per share. It quickly rose and within thirty days the price was at $19 per share. After struggling for years and hoping for an IPO, it finally happened and my "calculated risk" paid off. I will never forget the feeling I had of relief to be able to get back to zero . . . from $65,000+ in credit card debt when the IPO happened.

I left AMCC in March of 1999 to do an Internet startup, implementing an idea that was conceived by my friend Rob Harris and me in 1995. It started out as a seedling of an idea on a patio in New York in April of 1995. My friend Rob had a business focused on serving people with disabilities. He had an idea for a traveling tradeshow that would travel around the country and offer people with disabilities an opportunity to see, feel, and experience products that they normally wouldn't have access to prior to purchasing. It wasn't a totally new idea, but the company that was competing in this market left much to be desired.

I was the president of eBilities.com for the first six months while we built our team and infrastructure and while we searched for a more qualified CEO to run the business—one who was better qualified than I was.

We raised $3 million in venture capital funding, which came with the perfect CEO (part of the package that came with our VC funding) in October 1999, and we had our launch party shortly thereafter. While we were the first to raise money for this niche, we had several competitors and had spoken to a couple of them about joining forces prior to raising capital.

None of those discussions panned out, and a couple of our competitors attracted the attention of major venture capitalists and raised more millions than we had. It quickly became clear that our new CEO, who was commuting from Philadelphia, where his family was, to San Diego, where the eBilities.com office was located, did not have the passion that my partner and I did, and within three months the company we had built for four years was gone.

From 2001 to 2005, I was the managing director of the U.S. operations of UR Group. It was during that time that we set out to create a sales rep organization that would be able to provide European technology products to the U.S. market. We started with California and had plans to expand with our success. During those four years, I had a chance to learn about sales and the challenges associated with closing deals.

From 2005 to 2006, I ran Day Elevator and Lift, a New York-based company focused on selling, installing, maintaining, and supporting residential elevators, stair lifts, and wheelchair lifts.

From 2007 to 2010, I ran Southern States University and the International Academy of, both based in San Diego. During the three-year period, I took both of these schools through national accreditation through different accreditation bodies, and each had its own guidelines and criteria to meet. I left the educational field in September 2010, and that is when my Internet marketing journey really began.

Can you tell us a little bit about how you make money online?

Affiliate Marketing—I have sold Clickbank products and JVZoo products as an affiliate and made a few thousand dollars doing several different promotions. But I have found that, in general, as an affiliate marketer you make a few dollars per product as an affiliate marketer, and so to build a sustainable business you must sell hundreds or thousands of products per month.

I have found my success online using the "license rights" model, marketing entire portfolio(s) of products from best-of-class product developers/creators. I have learned that the best portfolio(s) to license are those that offer everything from an entry-level product all the way through to high-ticket (with high commission) products. The idea is that once you have a customer, why make them leave you when they are ready to take things to the next level? So, that is my criteria, and I highly recommend the "license rights" model, where you can shortcut the process you would have to go through to create your own product line. I have found this to be, by far, the best model for making a great living online while keeping your life relatively simple.

How did you get started in an online business?

Accidentally. I kept seeing ads and I clicked on one, got on an Internet marketer's list, and started reading his e-mail messages and watching his videos. I could see that this guy was not that smart—in fact, he was self-deprecating and would speak about the fact that if HE could do it, anyone could. I was tired of my job and my boss, and his story and message resonated with me. That being said, I really started doing Internet stuff back in 1993 and always had ideas for building an online business, including my Internet startup in 1999.

When did you first decide that an online business was right for you?

I am an engineer and have dabbled with online business opportunities for almost twenty years. But I never focused on making money online until the middle of 2011, and since then it has been quite an adventure. I first decided that an online business was for me after dabbling for six months, having left my job and the security that went with it. I explored many options, and by mid-2011 I knew that this was the best way for me to take control of my future.

How long did it take you to get you to where you are now, and what would you say to our readers who are just getting started?

All of my life's experiences have helped me to get to where I am now. With respect to Internet marketing, I invested a lot of time and money to learn the skills that I was lacking in order to achieve success online.

I have learned that to make money online requires three elements: 1) a proven financial model (the most crucial part of a complete business plan) that you believe in and hold yourself accountable to achieve; 2) a coach to give you direction, support, and a kick in the butt when you need it; and 3) a supportive community to be there when you need the support.

I have tried helping many people who are trying to get started, and it is very difficult to succeed when working with people who have a broken mindset. And nearly as challenging is helping people who have no money and are feeling desperate to have success in the timetable that they would need to achieve it.

What are the top three to five areas readers should concentrate on when starting off?

If you are serious about making this into a business, then here are the areas that you must focus on:

You must do your due diligence just as you would if you were buying a business, buying a franchise, or starting your own business. That includes creating a financial model that you can measure your performance against.

Choose the niche that you will focus on and research it very carefully. Start with the end in mind. That means knowing how you will monetize the business before you start investing any money into it. This echoes back to number one.

Choose one marketing strategy and get really good at it. Find a coach who knows how to succeed with that strategy, and follow exactly what the coach tells you to do.

Continuously test—it's all about testing analyzing and optimizing. The goal is to get more out than you put in, but that usually takes testing and optimization.

Can you recommend some quality resources for our readers, that have helped you?

I don't know what I would do without Google. You can find almost any answer today by just doing a simple Google search. Second only to Google is YouTube. For anything that you need to know how to do, you can do a quick YouTube search, watch a video, and you are empowered.

The search capability that is inherent in Gmail is so powerful and we take it for granted, but you can use that to find almost any message about any topic you exchange with anyone at any time. There is great power in knowing how to use simple features like that. I could tell you about many advanced tools that you can pay money for that start by using those that are right in front of you.

That includes Google Docs, which is now called Google Drive. You can do just about anything that you were able to do on Microsoft Office, but now you can do it on a shared virtual drive that you can have access to from anywhere and you can share with anyone and it just makes life so easy. We take things like that for granted, but I don't know how we lived without them.

An autoresponder is an essential tool in this business. A tool for creating simple lead pages or squeeze pages is also essential. It's all about creating irresistible offers, using great copy, and then following up with your prospects. So, tools that will help you achieve those objectives are worth their weight in gold.

What's your favorite way to drive traffic to your website?

The best way to drive traffic to my website, to your website, or to any offer out there is with paid traffic. So I'm not sure what you mean when you say what is your favorite way to drive traffic.

I guess my answer is that my favorite way is the way that provides the best return on my investment. And that doesn't mean just financial. My favorite way is the way that converts best.

Specific paid traffic methodologies include solo ads, banner ads, Facebook news feed ads and sidebar ads, as well as buying spots in targeted media, which is a variation of a banner ad. I use all of these methods of advertising. But the key to success with any advertising campaign or strategy is targeting the right audience—and then having the right targeted message, the right solution, and the right irresistible offer for that audience.

What are some pitfalls that our readers should be on the lookout for, and how can they be avoided?

Two of the top pitfalls are information overload and "shiny object syndrome."

Information overload starts with clicking on an offer, and before you know it your e-mail box is overloaded with one great offer after another. And each one comes with webinar training and further reading, and you realize that before you can do anything, you need to learn a lot more. And then you continue learning and learning and getting more overwhelmed because you realize there's more and more to do before you can do anything, and that is what stops many people from taking action. This information overload—not knowing which direction to turn and what is really important to know before really getting started—that is the fatal blow for many.

Shiny object syndrome happens because you're getting e-mail after e-mail from marketer after marketer, and every offer sounds better than the previous one. So you get into one opportunity and realize that it didn't work the way you thought it would, you didn't get rich in thirty days or less, and along comes another great offer in your e-mail box and you jump onto that opportunity, hoping that it will really be the one.

Another pitfall involves the challenges associated with working from home—the distractions, the lack of regimen or a boss or deadlines to meet. Many people need to have that structure in their day in order to feel productive and be the most successful.

What's the biggest mistake you made getting started?

I didn't have a financial model that I believed in. And that was ironic because I had written several business plans in the past and had run a university where I reviewed hundreds of business plans. Yet, when I started my Internet business I didn't do that. It seemed too abstract, too unpredictable, because I really didn't have a model that I had any confidence in. And your entire financial model in businesses is based on having assumptions that you believe in; I never felt that I had enough information to make those assumptions.

I spent tons of money on virtual assistants and on employees to execute the various plans I was working toward, but I didn't have a solid business model . . . and so as I was making progress in moving forward with my knowledge and expertise and my brand and reputation, I wasn't generating enough income to survive.

So the biggest mistake, really, was pursuing business models that I didn't have the confidence to put into a financial model. And as the results were not meeting the goals that I had in my head, I didn't take quick-enough corrective action.

When you don't know where you're going, that's exactly where you wind up.

What big mistakes do you see others make?

One of the biggest mistakes I've seen people make is investing all their money into creating a professional presence online and not having any money left to generate traffic. Continuous traffic is the lifeblood of your business.

The other big mistake people make is thinking that they can make money online without any money, because they hear stories about that happening. But what they don't realize is that there is always either (a) money spent to generate traffic or (b) time spent to create value, which will ultimately lead to organic traffic.

Many people fail because they don't have the work ethic to put in the focused time to learn what needs to be done and to then execute it on a daily basis to generate the traffic that they need—at no out-of-pocket cost. So "free" is really a misnomer, because that type of traffic requires time, hard work, and dedication, and most people are not willing to invest enough of each before they give up. People quit before they put in the time and effort to succeed.

What information do you wish you'd had when you were first starting out?

Let me start by saying that all the information that I'd wish I'd had—had been readily available to me. I just didn't know what to look for. Those reading this book are taking a great step toward success by learning from others who have gone before them. Combine that with a sense of urgency, a strong work ethic, and a focus on one thing, and you'll be way ahead of the game.

That being said, I wish that I'd worked more closely with someone (or even better, a group of people) who had already achieved the level of success that I was looking for, and that I had willed to follow their guidance, direction, and strategies.

I wish that I'd understood more about licensing programs and the best high-commission products available for licensing. Having a complete product line, ready to go, gives online marketing "new-bies," without experience or technical skills, the leverage to get jump-started in an online business while learning skills they can apply to their own product or business idea, which otherwise would be too overwhelming and intimidating to even consider.

What do you think are the keys to becoming a successful online?

One quality that everyone I know who is truly successful online shares is their passion for helping other people. The more people you help, the more money you make. That I have found to be especially true in the online world, where people are willing and happy to pay for the training that will help them achieve success.

Integrity, a willingness to help and to share, and a true love for what you do are common characteristics I have seen in people who are making money online.

And I believe that true success, whether online or offline, to be lasting success requires hard work, commitment, perseverance, and all of the qualities I have mentioned above.

I'm sure that most of those who fail to make money online fail because they don't possess these traits—or if they do, they just don't stick with it for long enough. It goes back to having a plan and sticking to it.

In your opinion, how can someone stand out among the competition?

The best way to stand out among the competition is to offer people value. You're not trying to be loved by everyone. It starts with defining your target audience, and then understanding them and understanding their problems, concerns, and issues.

The more you can help them to overcome their problems, to solve their problems, to help themselves, the more they will like you. When a prospect finds you and hears your message, he or she will not be hearing the same message from other people. If he or she happens to find you—and during that short moment, you stand out by proving you're real and approachable—that will make a difference. Provide your contact information and encourage people to contact you. I always do that. I include my phone number on most of my e-mails and always tell my prospects to contact me if they have questions.

Personal contact. Picking up the phone. In fact, one of the pieces of feedback that I get most often is how people are so surprised that I actually pick up the phone. They're amazed that it's really me on the other line, like I am a celebrity or something, and I hear the same thing from Internet marketers over and over again.

What are some things that you do NOT recommend for online entrepreneurs?

Don't promote your product online. Promote yourself. Online is a place where you can get people's attention and you can show them who you are, what you can do for them, and how you can help them. Show them how much you care. Until they know how much you care, they won't care what you know or about your product or about your offer of the day. On the other hand, once they know you, they will be much more receptive to following your every recommendation.

I don't suggest investing in courses or programs until you have a strategy in mind. I don't recommend selling affiliate products or MLM products, which require thousands of units be sold in order for you to make six figures per year. I don't recommend trying, or expecting, to get rich quick. Don't invest in a second program until completing the first program. I don't recommend going out and spending a lot of money on a new computer. You can get everything you need for under $500 used on Craigslist or in a similar classified medium.

And, of course, I don't recommend doing anything just to make money, online or offline, if it's unethical or illegal. There are plenty of legal, ethical, and exciting opportunities out there . . . so find one that appeals to you.

What's one of the things that you find most challenging about an online business?

It's difficult to stay focused on moneymaking activities. There are many distractions. Social media is so enticing—it's fun to chat and interact with your friends from around the world, and sometimes you can justify that this relationship is either paying you or that it will materialize into something more significant in the future. But without a specific plan, it won't.

Also, believing in yourself enough to stay on course when the money is not coming in and change course as needed. Most of the people in my life don't understand what I do and often have the perception that online businesses are scams, that I'm looking for the easy money, that I should just get a job like everyone else. It can be very deflating and de-motivating when these influences seem to be every-where in your world.

What's your favorite part of your day as an online marketer?

I get the most satisfaction from hearing my students' pleasure and satisfaction when I teach them new skills, and even more so when they start having their own success. I get a lot of satisfaction from teaching and helping others, but there is nothing that feels better to me than when my students (who tend to become my friends) start having success on their own.

What does it really take to succeed in business, in your opinion?

Hard work, commitment, and perseverance. In many ways, it's no different than succeeding in any other business. While you hear crazy success stories about people making crazy money in a matter of months, that is the exception. And when the exception is YOU, that can snowball into something you may not even imagine right now. But if you can believe it, you can achieve it. So it does help to have the vision and not to just accept the outcome based on circumstance. Most overnight success stories really take years of work and experi-ence to execute successfully.

If you had to share three to five keys to building a successful online business, what would they be in order of priority?

- Start with the end in mind.
- Create a business plan, especially a financial model, and review it with someone who understands business plans.
- Continuously measure, analyze, and optimize.
- Use outsourcing to leverage your limited time.
- Model successful marketers. There is no reason to reinvent the wheel.

For each of those keys, what are some goals that our readers should set for reaching each one of them?

Start with the end in mind—Know how much you want to make

and by when. Separate your business goals from your personal goals and at the same time consider the impact of one on the other. If your personal goals (i.e., time with family and friends, travel, independence) is consistent with your business goals, that's a great start. If you can incorporate your passion into your online business and the financial model works, fantastic! If not, consider a more "practical" solution for making money, and then you can leverage that money to pursue your passion in the future.

Create a business plan, especially a financial model—Know how much you have to invest and be sure that it's in line with your financial model. Be sure that you can live with the numbers that you include in the plan, and then commit to making sure you meet or exceed those numbers.

Continuously measure, analyze, optimize—Use click-tracking software, continually split test, analyze results, and optimize offers, funnels, and follow-ups.

Use outsourcing to leverage your limited time—Itemize your daily tasks between moneymaking activities and non-moneymaking activities, and outsource all non-moneymaking activities. Much of this can be done with virtual assistants who charge less than $10 per hour. In fact, there are many talented online marketers around the world who you can hire for less than $5 an hour, even as little as $3 an hour for full-time work. It's crazy, but they are out there in many countries including the Philippines, Pakistan, and India, and they are related to make this kind of money.

Model successful marketers—Go to events regularly to network and learn. That is where you can hear firsthand from the leaders exactly what they are doing . . . and from that the wheels start spinning and you will come up with your own variation on one of the ideas you saw presented there. Invest 20% of your time learning, specifically focus on what other marketers in your niche are doing to get ideas, and then model those you like. Continually monitor content and offers made by your favorite marketers for new ideas.

What are some realistic long-term and short-term goals for our readers?

Short-term as in ninety days, my recommendation is to spend

your time doing your due diligence so you can minimize your learning curve and your time traversing the school of hard knocks.

There are many options when it comes to making money online, and there is no reason to rush into choosing one or another without the proper education to make that choice. So I would not set an expectation to be making money in the first ninety days.

As for long-term goals, the sky's the limit. If you invest on the front in your education and continue to invest as you learn and implement strategies, there is no unrealistic goal that you can set for yourself. There are countless examples of online marketers making millions of dollars per year, using many strategies . . . but there are very few who make millions without investing time, effort, and money on the front and in order to achieve those results. I think it was Tim Ferriss who said it takes ten thousand hours to master a skill. Don't expect overnight success. With that mindset, there will come a time when your hard work pays off. Just don't expect that to be a short-term reality.

What's the first thing you recommend our readers do after they're done reading this book?

You can read all your life, but if you don't implement, you are wasting your time. The first thing I recommend is to think very hard about what the end game is for you. If that's not clear, it's worth investing time to figure it out before investing money in any tools or products to help you succeed online. So my recommendation is to start implementing, and the beginning of implementing is putting together your business plan. With a well-thought-out plan, you can save millions of dollars and years of your life that you might otherwise waste pursuing goals that are not clear or well-enough thought through.

Who are the people that inspired you and why?

Roberto Shinyashiki is a friend of mine. I have watched him write books and I took a course that he taught. He was the first one who told me that I needed to write a book. I give him the credit for my perseverance in this process. He is also the person who suggested that I would like T. Harv Ecker, who wrote *Secrets of the Millionaire Mind* and created the "Millionaire Mind Intensive," a three-day workshop that I would recommend to everyone as a place to get the right mindset for starting your own business. Zig Ziglar was probably the first motivational speaker who really resonated with me. I loved his book *How to Raise Positive Kids in a Negative World*. I admire and am inspired by Steve Jobs and Elon Musk, who have both demonstrated how it is possible to run multiple billion-dollar businesses simultaneously and still have a life.

What did you learn from those people, that you'd like to pass on to our readers?

Without the proper mindset, it is almost impossible to succeed. And many who do succeed without the proper mindset ultimately lose their wealth. Stinkin' thinkin' will destroy your dream as fast as you can dream it. On the other hand, if you believe it, you can achieve it. To get results, it starts with a desire that just won't quit. Praise success and don't criticize failure—and that includes not criticizing yourself too harshly for your own failures.

What tools/resources would you say are essential?

As I mentioned earlier, the only two tools that you need to get started are your Google search engine and YouTube. By searching on Google, you can find tools for just about every possible need you can identify. And most of them are free or extremely inexpensive to use in a limited fashion, and the power that you can get in the tools available today is absolutely amazing. On YouTube, you can get instructional training on just about anything you can imagine.

Once you have a business, an autoresponder is critical. This one tool alone gives you the ability to automatically stay in contact with your customers and prospects on an ongoing basis. But it's not just an autoresponder or one tool or another . . . it's an entire strategy that begins with the end in mind. Without that, you can have a toolbox full of tools that you never get around to using. I see it happen too often.

A simple camera for making videos becomes important once your business plan is defined and you know what you will be promoting. The camera built into your smartphone is more than adequate for getting started. By creating videos, people can get to know YOU . . . which is the way to start building "know, like, and trust." Production of those videos that include your beautiful face should be done by outsourcing to a video production expert for a few dollars an hour. Then you can move on to creating your next piece of content rather than being weighed down trying to make your finished product look professional, without the skills yourself to know where to begin.

What final words of wisdom would you like to pass on to everyone who's reading this chapter?

If you believe you can, you can. You have a strong desire, a burning desire, to take control of your life—you can do it and you MUST do it. Life is full of choices and decisions. If you like what you read in this book, I recommend that you make the decision to move forward with this business model. That means you are now ready to start thinking about what your business looks like when it's done.

As Steven Covey teaches in his book *The 7 Habits of Highly Successful People*, the first step is to start with the end in mind. Every leader in the online industry will tell you that you should model successful marketers. And it has never been easier to do so. There is so much great information available at your fingertips. Your competitors will give you lots of great information and ideas to get you started. The rest is up to you. Take the ideas you get from this book seriously, and incorporate the ones that resonate with you into your business plan and your personal life plan, and you will be miles ahead of 95% of the population.

Name: Tammy and Mike Morin

Where are you from?

We are from central California.

Former career (or present career if still working):

We are in the collateral lending business. We have over thirty employees and have been self-employed practically our entire lives.

Can you tell us a little bit about how you make money online?

We leverage systems that allow us to sell their products and services.

How did you get started in an online business?

Out of the necessity to live the lifestyle that we desire.

When did you first decide that an online business was right for you?

When we saw the opportunity of being able to do business wherever there was an Internet connection.

How long did it take you to get you to where you are now, and what would you say to our readers who are just getting started?

It took about a year and a half. And to a beginner, we would say, "Your income follows your skillsets! Learn the skills that are needed to create your online opportunity."

What are the top three to five areas readers should concentrate on when starting off?

Know your customer better than your product, be sure you know your what and why, and find a great mentor. With those three things, you'll have a solid foundation for any online business.

Can you recommend some quality resources for our readers, that have helped you?

YouTube is a great resource. You can find answers to most of your questions. Another of our favorite resources is www.danijohnson.com, and searching out podcasts on iTunes.

What's your favorite way to drive traffic to your website?

Paid traffic if you have the resources such as Facebook, pay-per-click, and cost-per-lead. If you don't have the resources, then YouTube (creating your own videos).

What are some pitfalls that our readers should be on the lookout for, and how can they be avoided?

Stay away from "Shiny Object Syndrome" and stay focused!

What's the biggest mistake you made getting started?

Grabbing at every business opportunity that came our way.

What big mistakes do you see others make?

They quit too early (quit before they make it).

What information do you wish you'd had when you were first starting out?

I wish someone would have told me to stay focused and not quit, but to go after what I wanted.

What do you think are the keys to becoming successful online?

Consistency and knowing your way!

In your opinion, how can someone stand out among the competition?

Be unique. Be you! You are going to attract the people who are attracted to you, so being someone else probably won't work for you.

What are some things that you do NOT recommend for online entrepreneurs?

I do not recommend believing that there's a magic button or website out there that's going to make you a ton of money.

What's one of the things that you find most challenging about an online business?

The time that you can waste online by being side-tracked by "shiny objects."

What's your favorite part of your day as an online marketer?

Helping others.

What does it really take to succeed in business, in your opinion?

Mindset and belief, personal growth and development, and action and implementation.

If you had to share three to five keys to building a successful online business, what would they be in order of priority?

- Find your niche.
- Know your customer.
- Build a list.
- Add value.
- Make an offer.

For each of those three to five keys, what are some goals that our readers should set for reaching each one of them?

- Do something that you desire—what interests you?
- Read the book *How to Win Friends and Influence People*.
- When building your list, take care of them like they're your babies.
- Added value speaks for itself. It's not always about taking; it's about giving back.
- With your offer, make sure it's a quality product.

What are some realistic long-term and short-term goals for our readers?

Within three to six months, you should expect to have made your first dollar. In the long-term, you should have your skill mastered, because, like I said earlier, your income follows your skillsets, so master them!

What's the first thing you recommend our readers do after they're done reading this book?

Implement. Take Action!

Who are the people that inspired you and why?

My wife! She never gave up on me and always told me to follow my dreams (Mike).

What did you learn from those people, that you'd like to pass on to our readers?

Do what you like, don't give up, and if you have a dream, take the steps to get there. Don't believe the lie that at a certain point in our lives we lose control of what is happening to us and our lives become controlled by fate.

What final words of wisdom would you like to pass on to everyone who's reading this chapter?

Every one of us has a genius inside of us. Go find it! (Mike). Don't let your fears stop you! Don't waste time—BE SCARED but do it anyway! (Tammy).

Name: Scott Ewart

Where are you from?

I was born in Southern California, but now I live in Winchester, Kentucky, just outside of Lexington.

Former career (or present career if still working):

I work for an IT company where I manage marketing corporate events for our customers and users.

Can you tell us a little bit about how you make money online?

I am primarily an affiliate marketer, where I promote other people's products and generate commissions for driving traffic that results in sales of those products.

How did you get started in an online business?

I read the book *Rich Dad, Poor Dad* and was inspired to create an alternative income to my 9–5 job. I wanted to protect myself and my family from losing my job and not having an alternative source of income or skills.

When did you first decide that an online business was right for you?

Once I started. I loved it because it was challenging, rewarding, and tapped into my past career as a computer programmer. It let me utilize a lot of those skills.

How long did it take you to get you to where you are now, and what would you say to our readers who are just getting started?

I have worked at this for over four years and have seen real success in the last year. I would say to others, research and find a successful mentor that has achieved what you are looking to do and follow them. Learn from them. Stick with it until it works. Don't jump around looking for the next shiny object that you think will make it happen for you. Also, it will not happen overnight. It takes work and perseverance, but it's worth the payoff in the end!

What are the top three to five areas readers should concentrate on when starting off?

Finding a good mentor, learning some basic skills for marketing, finding a good community, developing a marketing plan for a year (broken down by the week and day), and finding products/opportunities that are in line with your interests so you will stick with it!

Can you recommend some quality resources for our readers, that have helped you?

Yes, two books. *Magnetic Sponsoring* and *Think and Grow Rich*.

What's your favorite way to drive traffic to your website?

I use a combination of solo ads, Yahoo advertising, and Facebook and Twitter ads.

What are some pitfalls that our readers should be on the lookout for, and how can they be avoided?

Too many choices, training programs, and "latest things." Information overload of those things that you think will help you. Pick one strategy, master it until you get results, and then move on.

What's the biggest mistake you made getting started?

Spending too much time learning and not enough time executing on money-generating activities.

What big mistakes do you see others make?

Exactly the same thing—it's prevalent in this industry.

What information do you wish you'd had when you were first starting out?

How to convert traffic into sales, writing good e-mails, and how to close sales.

What do you think are the keys to becoming a successful online?

Having good focus, acquiring basic skills, finding and following a good mentor, mastering skills, and then teaching others how to get those same skills.

In your opinion, how can someone stand out among the competition?
Provide value to others and don't push your business or links onto someone else.

What are some things that you do NOT recommend for online entrepreneurs?
Giving up. Never give up. It may take some time, but there is money to be made and success to be had.

What's one of the things that you find most challenging about an online business?
Staying focused on projects, not getting distracted by lots of training and products. Online marketers are prime targets for those that make products, so be careful what you choose to buy, and if you do, execute on it!

What's your favorite part of your day as an online marketer?
In the morning, when I execute on my daily activities and check my results.

What does it really take to succeed in business, in your opinion?
Persistence, knowledge, execution, and a good mentor.

If you had to share three to five keys to building a successful online business, what would they be in order of priority?
Focus, Mentor, Accountability, Tracking, Execution.

For each of those keys, what are some goals that our readers should set for reaching each one of them?
Focus—Pick something and stick with it. Don't wander off and keep trying new things. Do your research first and give it a solid three months of effort before you throw in the towel and try something else.

Mentor—Research and find a good mentor who wants to teach you and give value to you. Then the key is to listen to them and follow what they teach, even if you think you know better!

Accountability—Find someone who is doing the same thing as you, at the same level. Work together and hold each other accountable for execution and staying focused.

Tracking—Start and keep a spreadsheet. Passwords, programs, advertising spent, and results of the advertising. Make sure you are making more than you are spending on advertising, and you will only know that from tracking.

Execution—Create a marketing plan, set daily and weekly goals, and stick with them. Don't get distracted by other things while in the middle of your plan. Execute on moneymaking activities first, then you can do other things.

What are some realistic long-term and short-term goals for our readers?

Short-term, find your way to making money and learning the basics. Long-term, have systems in place that will be making you money even if you're not working. If you take two weeks' vacation, you want your systems working for you and revenue still coming in, not something you have to hand-hold every day.

What's the first thing you recommend our readers do after they're done reading this book?

Just go do it. Don't procrastinate. Jump right in and just do it.

Who are the people that inspired you and why?

I'm inspired by anyone who has the guts to stick with it and make it happen for themselves. Some notables are Mike Dillard, Matt Lloyd, and Vince Reed. My father inspired me by working so hard all his life to provide a good life for his family and my mother after he was gone.

What did you learn from those people, that you'd like to pass on to our readers?

Providing value, perseverance, and wanting to help other people succeed.

What final words of wisdom would you like to pass on to everyone who's reading this chapter?

Jump in and do it, keep learning, stay focused, track and celebrate your successes, and be your own cheerleader when no one else will.

Name: Hamilton Powell

Where are you from?

Atlanta, Georgia

Former career (or present career if still working):

I am the Founder/CEO of Crown & Caliber.

What is your website(s)?

http://www.crownandcaliber.com/

Can you tell us a little bit about how you make money online?

Crown & Caliber is the preferred solution for selling a luxury watch. Our consignment service allows us to help customers sell their watches for the highest possible price. Using our network of over forty thousand watch enthusiasts and collectors, as well as over three hundred domestic and international dealers, our website, e-mail blasts, and other various sites, our watches get in front of thousands of eyes, ensuring that we get the highest possible price for each watch.

How did you get started in an online business?

When I was looking for ideas on what kind of company to create, I began researching the different items that one could sell online. That was when I realized that there was no great way to sell a luxury watch online. I knew that creating an online company where people could sell their luxury watches was the best decision because it met the needs of the market.

When did you first decide that an online business was right for you?

Our first customer sold a Rolex Oysterquartz with us. When I saw the joy on his face when he was told the ultimate selling price, I knew we had a great service. It was then that we got serious about growing the business.

How long did it take you to get you to where you are now, and what would you say to our readers who are just getting started?

Crown & Caliber is two years old and we are growing at a very rapid pace. For people who are just starting a new online business, it is important to be patient. Growth at the beginning will be slow, but once you are able to amend your processes to be efficient as possible, you will begin to see growth.

What are the top three to five areas readers should concentrate on when starting off?

One of the most important aspects to concentrate on when starting off a new business is the company culture. It is important to establish the foundation core values of your business and stress them to our employees.

After determining these core company values, it is important to hire people who will abide by these important company fundamentals.

Another important area to concentrate on is customer service. Without customers, you will have no business, so it is imperative that their experience with your company is at the top of your mind at all times. Set up systems and processes that make their time working with you pleasant, easy, and rewarding.

Can you recommend some quality resources for our readers, that have helped you?

The best thing I can recommend is to read—and read often. Don't become a silo. Reading will elevate your standards.

What's your favorite way to drive traffic to your website?

Our team spends a lot of time creating quality watch-related content. We have recently launched a Watch Style Guide that includes a wide range of topics, such as watch reviews and how-to guides. Many watch enthusiasts have found these articles to be very interesting and informative, and have shared them via social media.

What are some pitfalls that our readers should be on the lookout for, and how can they be avoided?

Just because your business is online doesn't mean that real-world business practices are inapplicable. Don't think you can avoid the rules of business. No matter how many e-commerce success stories you hear that are seemingly centered around "build it and they will come," you can't think like that.

What's the biggest mistake you made getting started?

One of the most important things that I have learned with Crown & Caliber is that it's not enough to just be better; you must be different. In the beginning, we thought that if we were quicker and offered higher prices than our competitors, that would be enough. Although we did achieve success with that mentality, I knew that there was more we could do. That's why we started our consignment process. This is something that no one else in the market is doing and we have had great success with the new process.

What big mistakes do you see others make?

One of the biggest mistakes that people make when starting an online business is offering a service or product that no one needs or wants. Just because you build something, it doesn't automatically mean that people will come. It's important to study the market before determining what product or service you will offer.

What information do you wish you'd had when you were first starting out?

It's better to create than to compete. I learned that through one of the best books I have ever read, *Blue Ocean Strategy*.

What do you think are the keys to becoming a successful online?

Some of the most important keys to becoming a successful online business is the ability to adapt and learn. We are constantly perfecting our processes in order to make them more efficient and convenient for the customer. We refuse to remain stagnant, knowing that there is always something more that we can do to make the customer's experience more rewarding. Also, I do my best to learn as much as I can.

I speak with executives in other industries to learn from their experiences and to figure out how they can applied to Crown & Caliber. I also study new trends in the industry so we can stay as up to date as possible.

In your opinion, how can someone stand out among the competition?

One great way to stand out among the competition is by the way your business treats its customers. At Crown & Caliber, we strive to make the process as rewarding and safe as possible for our customers. We do our best to deliver every quote through a phone call rather than just an e-mail so that we can learn more about the customer and assure them that we have their best interests in mind. Customers are always thanking us for updating them at every step in our process, and, at the end of our transaction, they tell us how easy and enjoyable the whole process was for them. I believe this white-glove treatment is what helps to set us apart from our competitors.

What are some things that you do NOT recommend for online entrepreneurs?

Don't just pick any product or service on which to build a company. It is important to pick something you're knowledgeable and passionate about. There needs to be a need for the product/service AND you need to have a passion for it.

Another thing that online entrepreneurs shouldn't do is set too-high expectations. Your business will not become a success overnight, and, more often than not, it can take months or years for it to take-off. Talk with other successful online entrepreneurs and learn about their experiences. These conversations can help you create realistic timelines and goals.

What's one of the things that you find most challenging about an online business?

Because there is no storefront with an online business, we do not get to speak with our customers face to face. As a result, some customers can be a bit skeptical and it can be difficult to establish trust. We do our best to speak with every customer on the phone, which gives us the opportunity to develop a relationship with them and to assure them that our processes are secure.

What's your favorite part of your day as an online marketer?
Interacting with customers is always enjoyable. It is very interesting to learn both their life story and the story of their timepiece.

What does it really take to succeed in business, in your opinion?
Ultimately the word "business" really is defined as a collection of people attempting to achieve a common objective. So "business" is really about people. So the thing I believe is most central to success is a genuine care for people.

If you had to share three to five keys to building a successful online business, what would they be in order of priority?
Patience—Your company is not going to take off overnight. Give it some time.

Adaptability—Be willing to adapt your processes to make them more efficient.

Passion—Because a lot of your time will be devoted to this company, it is important to be passionate about the business.

What's the first thing you recommend our readers do after they're done reading this book?
If you haven't already started an online company, then the first thing you need to do is to find a product/service for which there is a need. If you have already started your business, it is important to hire people who will share the same vision for your company that you have for it.

Who are the people that inspired you and why?
One of my favorite books is one on the concept of "work" and is called Every Good Endeavor by Tim Keller. He is definitely an inspiration for me for a lot of reasons.

What did you learn from those people, that you'd like to pass on to our readers?
The concept of responsibility vs. control. At the end of the day,

entrepreneurs are no different from farmers. We all have a responsibility to work hard and do the right things. Like a farmer, we are supposed to plant, toil, harvest, etc. There are certain things we have a responsibility to do—otherwise, our business will fail. But also like a farmer, we ultimately have zero control over our success. We have no control over whether it "rains" or not.

That concept has made the low times more manageable and the high times more humbling.

What tools/resources would you say are essential to growing?

Books. Lots of books. Read, read, read.

What final words of wisdom would you like to pass on to everyone who's reading this chapter?

Being an entrepreneur is not for everyone—but for those chosen few, I encourage you to view your business as a vehicle for more than just achieving financial success.

Name: Nicole Snow

Where are you from?
Jackson, New Jersey

Former career (or present career if still working):
Officer in the Air Force, worked in contracting—wrote contracts between small businesses and the air force base.

What is your website(s)?
www.darngoodyarn.com

Can you tell us a little bit about how you make money online?
Sell multiple channels of recycled silk yarn, craft supplies, notions, etc.

How did you get started in an online business?
My husband's job kept moving all around the country, and I really wanted to start a business and online was the only option.

When did you first decide that an online business was right for you?
First business: 2006—wanted to get back to making art, wanted to move to that realm. DGY started April 2008.

How long did it take you to get you to where you are now, and what would you say to our readers who are just getting started?
I controlled my own growth because of my own circumstances with constantly moving around the country, so it took longer to "grow up" in terms of cash flow—but I learned lots along the way.

My advice: Learn every process, then learn how to delegate those processes. From packing orders, to doing customer service. Keep focused on the things only you can truly do for your business.

What are the top three to five areas readers should concentrate on when starting off?

Family support—Even if they aren't supporting you financially, they are critical shareholders because of the time and support they give.

How many hours can you truly devote to your business?

I put in sixteen-hour days pretty regularly.

Have a higher purpose. Other people relying on your business, supporting others in need. Bring in a more big and beautiful picture of what the business is, not just buying and selling on the Internet.

Can you recommend some quality resources for our readers, that have helped you?

Podcasts, "Accidental Creative"

Inc. magazine

Audible, listening to business books—"Delivering Happiness"

What's your favorite way to drive traffic to your website?

Social media—Facebook & Pinterest.

https://www.facebook.com/DGYarn

http://www.pinterest.com/darngoodyarn/

What are some pitfalls that our readers should be on the lookout for, and how can they be avoided?

Shady SEO companies that promise crazy results—you can get yourself banned from Google by using SEO incorrectly. Avoid "get rich quick" type sites.

What's the biggest mistake you made getting started?

Hiring the wrong people, having unrealistic expectations of what people can do for the business, and not realizing that friends don't always make the best employees.

What big mistakes do you see others make?

Not connecting with their customers—just trying to use them as

ATM machines. The purpose of social media is to connect and really take an interest in your customer. Making long-term relationships. We have a 45%-return business base because we make that connection.

What information do you wish you'd had when you were first starting out?

Part of the process is learning. I like where I started and where I've ended up. I've enjoyed the process of learning, screwing things up, and then getting them right the next time.

What do you think are the keys to becoming a successful online?

Learn everything you can about social and digital marketing.

In your opinion, how can someone stand out among the competition?

Provide connection with their customer.

What are some things that you do NOT recommend for online entrepreneurs?

Doing something without putting everything into it. You need to give something your full attention. If you can't do that, the timing or business isn't right for you.

What's one of the things that you find most challenging about an online business?

Time! There's always something else to do, there's always something else to learn—it gets a little intense sometimes. You need to be doing something you are really passionate about or you could easily be overrun.

What's your favorite part of your day as an online marketer?

Seeing comments when we put up new patterns or new content on the site.

What does it really take to succeed in business, in your opinion?

Passion and drive.

If you had to share three to five keys to building a successful online business, what would they be in order of priority?

Defining your customer segment.

Figuring out what channel you are going to use to reach them.

Perfecting those channels—in my case, making it an amazing website.

Creating a strategic marketing plan to target that segment.

Continuing to revise all of those steps as you learn more—it's all about the customer.

For each of those keys, what are some goals that our readers should set for reaching each one of them?

I would set goals in terms of revenue you want to reach, while taking into account what your expenditures are and what kind of business model you are using.

What are some realistic long-term and short-term goals for our readers?

Profitability in eighteen months, and if not, you should re-figure your business model. Maintaining extremely low overhead for the first three years of operation. Having a repeat customer base—at least 30%–35% should be repeat customers.

What's the first thing you recommend our readers do after they're done reading this book?

Get a business model canvas and define who the customer is—then fill in the rest of the canvas.

Who are the people that inspired you and why?

Rob Dyrdek (Professional skateboarder/entrepreneur)—He is super successful, but there is also an element of fun and being true to his core values.

My family—To keep me on the straight and narrow. People who own businesses tend to isolate, and my family helps me keep my priorities in check. They help me remember it's not only all about making money.

What did you learn from those people, that you'd like to pass on to our readers?

Have fun, and keep your priorities in check.

What final words of wisdom would you like to pass on to everyone who's reading this chapter?

Trust your gut, fire fast, and have fun.

Name: Scott Jordan

Where are you from?

Chicago, Illinois

Former career (or present career if still working):

Lawyer

What is your website(s)?

www.scottevest.com

Can you tell us a little bit about how you make money online?

By selling 40+ products that are engineered with hidden pockets for the everyday traveler.

How did you get started in an online business?

My wife, Laura, was tired of carrying everything for me, but the only things on the market with tons of pockets were fishing or photography vests with bulky exterior pockets. I knew there was a better way to carry all my things and so I received a patent for wiring headphones and batteries through clothing. We license that technology to other companies as TEC-Technology Enabled Clothing®. While waiting for the patent, I started www.SCOTTEVEST.com, the first clothing brand launched online.

When did you first decide that an online business was right for you?

When I knew that I wanted to launch a clothing company for everyone to be able to take advantage of my products with hidden pockets. Doing so online gave me a global reach.

How long did it take you to get you to where you are now, and what would you say to our readers who are just getting started?

This has been a thirteen-year journey. I would say not to let others set your bar. Set your own bar and aim ten feet above it!

What are the top three to five areas readers should concentrate on when starting off?

Focus on meeting the needs of consumers, dedicating time for PR, and connecting with customers through social media.

Can you recommend some quality resources for our readers, that have helped you?

Peter Shankman is an excellent resource for all things business and marketing. He has some really good books and articles with tips on PR, customer service, and management.

What's your favorite way to drive traffic to your website?

Social media. Reaching out to customers via Twitter, Facebook, etc. Also, creating fan events for customers and attending trade shows.

What are some pitfalls that our readers should be on the lookout for, and how can they be avoided?

Imitation is the sincerest form of flattery; however, when it comes to copycats, our products were stolen from AyeGear and our company has been in litigation with them for years now because of this.

What's the biggest mistake you made getting started?

Not creating a stronger company corporate culture until later on.

What big mistakes do you see others make?

They do not have the attitude to "figure it out!"

What information do you wish you'd had when you were first starting out?

What do you think are the keys to becoming a successful online?

Reaching out to customers and creating relationships with those customers. Constantly innovating and updating the online customer experience.

In your opinion, how can someone stand out among the competition?

Providing quality products and good customer service as a standard daily practice. To really grab attention from customers, having a creative and out-of-the-box social media campaign will put you above your competition.

What are some things that you do NOT recommend for online entrepreneurs?

Don't undervalue quality IT professionals. For example, when my Shark Tank episode aired, we weren't properly prepared and our site crashed.

What's one of the things that you find most challenging about an online business?

Not being able to see and interact with your customers on a day-to-day basis. Getting to know them on a personal level takes more effort.

What's your favorite part of your day as an online marketer?

Social media.

What does it really take to succeed in business, in your opinion?

Creating customers for life!

If you had to share three to five keys to building a successful online business, what would they be in order of priority?

Find the right outlets and channels to reach your specific customer base.

Have an innovative online customer experience including multiple ways to access customer service.

You can never have too much information or photos about your products online since customers can't actually see them.

Go above and beyond for your customers.

For each of those keys, what are some goals that our readers should set for reaching each one of them?

Set your own bar for achievement and figure it out!

What's the first thing you recommend our readers do after they're done reading this book?

Buy a SCOTTEVEST!

Who are the people that inspired you and why?

My wife. We started our business together and couldn't have done it without each other.

What final words of wisdom would you like to pass on to everyone who's reading this chapter?

Don't take no for an answer!

Name: Billy Thompson

Where are you from?

Grew up in Carlisle, Pennsylvania. Been in SoCal for twelve years—Los Angeles for eight years, now San Diego but possibly moving to Anaheim Hills in April to be closer to our office (our warehouse/fulfillment is located in Placentia, California).

Former career (or present career if still working):

Former: Private jet sales.

What is your website(s)?

www.thompsontee.com

Can you tell us a little bit about how you make money online?

Through our website and Amazon, we sell a patent-pending undershirt that blocks underarm sweat for men and women.

How did you get started in an online business?

We wanted to test our product/market, so starting online was logical. We were focused on big-box retailers, gaining interest from Men's Wearhouse, Macys, Nordstrom, Neiman Marcus, Bloomingdales, and Saks. We tested our product in the antiperspirant aisle of Rite Aid (didn't go well). Given all the risk associated with big-box retail and the success we've had online, we're now going strictly online with no plans to go brick-and-mortar retail.

When did you first decide that an online business was right for you?

See above answer.

How long did it take you to get you to where you are now, and what would you say to our readers who are just getting started?

As a bootstrapped business (we turned down investment offers requiring us to move production overseas—proudly, our product is handcrafted in the USA), we had to sink all the revenue back into the company to keep up with demand. We just passed the magical two-year mark in January (so banks will finally extend us credit) and the business finally has enough working capital to keep up with a growing company and pay us a good salary.

My advice to anyone starting out is save the most money you can, keep your credit in good standing, and have perseverance. If you truly believe in your idea/business (oftentimes you'll be the only one who does), then go all-in to give yourself an honest chance at success—because it doesn't matter what business you're starting, self-funded or not, it's going to be hard. It has to by nature or else everyone would be doing it. Remember that key point—it has to be hard.

What are the top three to five areas readers should concentrate on when starting off?

Cash Flow—Cash is king, and without you can't really do anything.

Operations—Make sure you're set up to provide your product/service in an efficient, scalable manner.

Marketing—Get the word out and find your customers. Internet marketing today has evened the playing field, allowing a start-up to compete with big business. Again, it won't be easy, but it's more possible now to compete than any time in history.

Your team (professional and personal)—Seek out other entrepreneurs or other free resources to use (SCORE). Have supportive personal relationships. My wife has been a huge supporter, and without her support, none of this would be possible.

Can you recommend some quality resources for our readers, that have helped you?

SCORE—free.

SBDC—free.

SBA.

Web—Just search your challenges, someone else probably went through it and wrote about it.

Accounting software—We use Quickbooks.

Inbound Marketing—This is Internet marketing 2.0.

What's your favorite way to drive traffic to your website?

For us it's national PR. We were featured on the show The Doctors and editor's pick in Shape magazine. Other ways include blog features, SEO, linkbacks, and social media.

What are some pitfalls that our readers should be on the lookout for, and how can they be avoided?

Don't underestimate based on your personal experience. For example, we didn't offer PayPal for the first year because neither I nor my biz partner used it. Now one-third of our business pays by Pay-Pal. The same goes for Amazon; we didn't want to offer anything on Amazon because we had our own site so why give Amazon a cut. Big mistake—Amazon is a rockstar for us.

What's the biggest mistake you made getting started?

Thinking we could go big-box retail right away. For anyone who's dealt with big-box, it's risky and most new, self-funded business most likely aren't ready.

What big mistakes do you see others make?

Honestly, no time or mental bandwidth to recall mistakes from others. I'm sure I came across many of them, as I like to read about business in general. Most recent mistake was from an article in Inc. magazine, where the founders of a controversial product antagonized the Federal Government—NEVER ANTAGONIZE THE FEDERAL GOVERNMENT.

Here's another one: Not focusing on your sales, customer service, growth, and scalability because all the other "stuff" doesn't really matter.

What information do you wish you'd had when you were first starting out?

Inbound marketing
Big box retail experience

What do you think are the keys to becoming a successful online?

Mastering inbound marketing—it's the way people shop online these days.

In your opinion, how can someone stand out among the competition?

Aside from the obvious competitive advantages, creating compelling/remarkable content for the web so customers can find and trust you.

What are some things that you do NOT recommend for online entrepreneurs?

Not understanding the inbound marketing concepts. Everything in e-commerce is trackable, so no need to "guess" at what's working.

What's one of the things that you find most challenging about an online business?

Mastering inbound marketing. Coming up with compelling content for the web. Competing against brick-and-mortar in terms of shipping delivery times and exchanges.

What's your favorite part of your day as an online marketer?

Reading new life-changing testimonials!

What does it really take to succeed in business, in your opinion?

Perseverance, intelligence, and a little luck!

If you had to share three to five keys to building a successful online business, what would they be in order of priority?

Your website—Easy to use and, more importantly, easy to buy! Inbound marketing.

Great customer service. This is fairly easy to do since most online retailers are poor at responding to customers/prospects, which has lowered the bar; thus, if you actually respond same day, customers are impressed.

For each of those keys, what are some goals that our readers should set for reaching each one of them?

Your website—Try it and have others try it, then get their feedback.

Inbound Marketing—There are many tools that will grade your site for this (i.e., http://marketing.grader.com/).

Great Customer Service—You'll know based on feedback.

What are some realistic long-term and short-term goals for our readers?

Short Term—Survival. Professionally and personally. One day at a time.

Long Term—Establishing an efficient, scalable business that will provide a product/service while generating personal wealth (not just income but business worth in the event of an acquisition).

What's the first thing you recommend our readers do after they're done reading this book?

Share it with all your social networks!

Who are the people that inspired you and why?

Michael Jordan—Cut from his high school basketball team.

Bill Gates and Steve Jobs—Made the personal computer what it is today despite all the naysayers in the beginning.

Sara Blakely—Founder of Spanx, 100% owner and youngest self-made female billionaire. We think we could emulate her success with our specialized garment.

What did you learn from those people, that you'd like to pass on to our readers?

Perseverance—you have to believe in yourself or else no one else will EVER believe in you.

What final words of wisdom would you like to pass on to everyone who's reading this chapter?

Believe, be smart, be creative, seek help, persevere, and remember it has to be hard or everyone else would be doing it. And lastly, the Golden Rule, treat others how you want to be treated.

Name: David Dutton

Where are you from?
Murfreesboro, Tennessee, but live outside of Nashville now.

Former career (or present career if still working):
I have never had a real job. I did work some college jobs while getting my business off the ground.

What is your website(s)?
www.MostConnectedMarketer.com and www.MarketingResults-Guaranteed.com are two of them.

Can you tell us a little bit about how you make money online?
I make a living selling my own products such as e-books, and I also sell affiliate products as well. I do take on a certain amount of consulting clients as well to help them market their business.

How did you get started in an online business?
I was attending Bible college in Chattanooga, Tennessee, and had already started a business while in college. I was fascinated by the Internet, though, and heard about people making money online.

I began to research ways to make money online, which led me to affiliate marketing. I joined a program by Marlon Sanders to promote his products. I will never forget it. I made $47 one day when I checked my e-mail. Overnight, I had sold one of Marlon's e-books and made $47. I never talked to anyone and couldn't even tell you who bought the e-book, but I got the credit. I was hooked after that!

When did you first decide that an online business was right for you?
Right after I made that first commission check.

How long did it take you to get you to where you are now, and what would you say to our readers who are just getting started?

It took me a lot longer than it would now because technology has made it much simpler than it was back in 2002. I worked on it for years and was making part-time money. Now, you can do it much quicker.

I would say to treat it like a business and stay focused. There are a million things online that will try to distract you from your goal.

What are the top three to five areas readers should concentrate on when starting off?

Picking the right business for you, building traffic to your site, building an e-mail list, and lastly, making offers to that list.

Can you recommend some quality resources for our readers, that have helped you?

I could name a ton, but I think anything by Jimmy D. Brown is great and I love Jonathan Leger.

What's your favorite way to drive traffic to your website?

Video marketing on YouTube.

What are some pitfalls that our readers should be on the lookout for, and how can they be avoided?

I would say one of the pitfalls people fall for is "the grass is greener" in some other business. Don't fall for it. All businesses have challenges. Pick one and stick to it for at least a year before you give up.

What's the biggest mistake you made getting started?

Easy question. I wasn't focused in the beginning. The older I got, the more focused I became. My income started going up as well.

What big mistakes do you see others make?

Another mistake that I see others make is not focusing on items that make you money. Sharpening pencils and straightening papers doesn't usually lead to someone paying you money.

What information do you wish you'd had when you were first starting out?

I wish I'd hired a mentor to help me sort out the good, bad, and ugly. Information is everywhere. It can be overwhelming. I think people like Deborah Robertson are great resources because people like her can help get someone started quickly.

What do you think are the keys to becoming a successful online?

I think someone must have a big reason why they are starting an online business to begin with. That is what will keep them going through the hard times.

I think it is crucial to only work on income-producing activities. This takes being honest with oneself and asking the tough questions. Is this what I should be working on right now?

In your opinion, how can someone stand out among the competition?

There is a lot more competition now than there ever has been, but many people don't take their brand or business seriously enough to worry about it.

Start with a great website design and branding. In the real world, people do judge a book by its cover, so you want to make sure your brand looks awesome. Just doing that alone will put a person miles ahead of the competition.

What's one of the things that you find most challenging about an online business?

Sometimes things are out of your control, such as Google making changes to their search engine (which impacted website rankings). You can either quit or learn to adapt. It is frustrating, but that's how the game is played.

What's your favorite part of your day as an online marketer?

Well, for me I like early morning to work on my business. It isn't something that I hate doing, so I do think it is my favorite part of the day.

What does it really take to succeed in business, in your opinion?

It comes down to character. Are you willing to do what it takes to start a real business online?

If you had to share three to five keys to building a successful online business, what would they be in order of priority?

I mentioned this before, but there are three areas one should master if they want to succeed online. They are traffic building, building a list, and lastly, selling things to that list.

For each of those keys, what are some goals that our readers should set for reaching each one of them?

Work on building up to a hundred visitors per day to your site. Next, go for five hundred and then go for one thousand unique visitors per day to your website.

While you are in the process, work on increasing the number of people on your mailing list. The more the better.

Lastly, get good at learning to sell to people. Improve your sales process. Focus on one sale and then another.

What's the first thing you recommend our readers do after they're done reading this book?

I would suggest they write down all the reasons why they want to start an online business and then hang it on a wall in their office. It all starts in the mind.

Who are the people that inspired you and why?

Tough question. There are a million people. Here are some of the people who inspired me and helped me along the way. Each person on this list is worth a Google search.

Jay Abraham
Dan Kennedy
Gary Halbert
Ben Settle
Jimmy D. Brown
David Frey

Napoleon Hill
John D. Rockefeller
Michael Senoff

What did you learn from those people, that you'd like to pass on to our readers?

Most of the people on this list are marketers. Very good marketers. I have learned a ton from all these people, and each person on this list has had a direct result in my income increasing over the years.

What final words of wisdom would you like to pass on to everyone who's reading this chapter?

I want to encourage everyone to not to let fear hold them back. Just get started. I know Deborah is a great resource to go to if someone isn't sure how to get started. Take advantage of that. Reach out to her.

About The Author

Deborah H. Robertson lives in Covington, Georgia, the same city where she was born and raised. She, too, has found a way to create a "plan b" income for herself using the Internet.

She comes from a large family, and she and her siblings and almost every grandchild in her family was brought up working in the family restaurant (Henderson's Restaurant) known for its catfish and hushpuppies. She credits her father and mother for providing her with the guidance that developed her strong work ethic, sound family values, and her abiding faith.

www.ingramcontent.com/pod-product-compliance
Lightning Source LLC
Chambersburg PA
CBHW051724170526
45167CB00002B/784